Non-Verbal Alchemy

Understand Hidden Communication

Termina Ashton

Copyright © 2018 by Termina Ashton
All rights reserved. No part of this book may be reproduced, scanned, or distributed in any printed or electronic form without permission.
First Edition: April 2018
ISBN- 13: 978-0-9954076-2-6

PerpelFlame P.I.M.P Publications 2018. PerpelFlame P.I.M.P Publications does not participate in, endorse, or have any authority or responsibility concerning private business arrangements between our authors and the public.

This book is designed to provide information and inspiration to readers. It is sold with the understanding that the author is not engaged to render any type of psychological, legal, or any other kind of professional advice. The content of each article is the sole expression and opinion of its author. No warranties or guarantees are expressed or implied by the author's choice to include any of the content in this volume. While all attempts have been made to verify information provided in this publication, the author assumes no responsibility for errors, omissions, or contrary interpretation of the subject matter herein. Any perceived slights of specific persons, peoples, or organizations are unintentional. The author shall have no liability or responsibility to any person or entity regarding physical, medical, psychological, emotional, financial, commercial damages, special, incidental, or consequential by the information contained in this book.

CONTENTS

Preface..7
Introduction...9
Chapter 1..13
- What is Body Language?
- Why is Body Language Essential Knowledge?
- The Mastermind and Incantation
- Energy Inoculation
- Automatic Body Language

Chapter 2..25
Fundamentals of body language
- The Fortune Teller
- Mind Strings
- First Impressions
- Reading People
- Why the Body Never Lies
- Observe Signals as a Group
- Consider Context
- Four Keystones
- The Dishonest and Honest Body

Chapter 3..45
Nature of People
- Introverts and Extroverts
- Body Language and Age
- Grooming
- Clothing
- Virtual Reality

Chapter 4..54
The Basics in Body Language
- Observe Incongruent Behaviours
- Get Your Desired Results
- Body English
- Pay Attention to Non-verbal Signals
- Tone of Voice
- Eye Contact
- Ask Questions
- Effective and Meaningful Communication
- Signals Can be Misread
- Conscious Practice
- Intuition and Perception
- Silent Speech Flow
- Environment and Conditioned Belief

- Obstruction of time
- Posture Expression
- Touch In Communication
- Pattern Interrupt and The Downtime Buffer

Chapter 5...83
Opened Mind, Closed Mind
- Abdominal Defence
- Hands And Palms
- Arms And Legs
- Ankle Cross
- Hand Lock and Four leg Cross
- The Fig Leaf
- Parallel Legs
- Pigeon Toes
- Hidden Standing Positions
- Releasing Our Guard
- Eyes
- Fetal Position
- Openness And Status

Chapter 6...110
Foundation Of Body Language
- Comfort/Discomfort
- Comfort and Discomfort Signal
- Illuminating and Activating Words
- Less IS More
- Deception Detection
- Guide to Comfort/Discomfort
- Acting on Discomfort Signals

Chapter 7...138
Your body Language
- Beacon Body
- When Your Body Language And Your Words Don't Coordinate
- Magic Of Self-Awareness
- Authenticity To Yourself and Others
- Self-Honesty
- Bulls#*t Fear
- The Vibrational Body
- Transmute Energy

Chapter 8 162
Interpret Facial Expressions
- Eyes
- Eye Trick to Predict
- Mouth
- Honest Smile and Shrugs

Chapter 9 191
Faking and Micro Expressions
- Breathing

Chapter 10 194
Posture and Personal Space
- Posture
- Personal Space
- Gestures
- Arms and Legs

Chapter 11 199
Reading the Signs
- Signals indicating interest
- Signals indicating that a person is more open to agree with you
- How to know if a person is thinking
- Signals indicating frustration or dismay
- How action-oriented people act or move
- How to know if a person is keeping a secret. Defensive/Hiding Something
- Signals indicating boredom
- Signals conveying excitement
- Signals exhibiting authority or power
- Body movements that signal anger and resistance
- Body movements that signal nervousness or tension.
- How to know if a person is having suspicions of you
- Signals when someone requires reassurance
- Indications of pride
- How to detect a liar
- Avoid jumping to conclusions

Chapter 12 211
Automatic Psychological States
- Dysphoria
- Normopathy
  Repetition compulsion
- Group feelings

Chapter 13 213
Subconscious Mirroring
- Correspond with moods
- Intentional Mirroring Practices
- Synchronicity and Remote Mirroring
- Mirroring And Smiling

Chapter 14 225
Body Language in Negotiations
- Power of First Impression
- Use your Body Language Knowledge
- Personal Space Negotiation

Chapter 15 228
Body Language in Selling

Chapter 16 234
Body Language in Job Interviews
- Leave a lasting impression
- Punctuality
- First Encounter
- Body Posture
- Gestures
- Eye Contact
- Panel Interview
- Interviewers Body Language
- Being Nervous is Okay

Chapter 17 240
Body Language in Meetings
- -Eye Contact

Chapter 18 243
Heart-To-Heart Body Language

Chapter 19 244
Body Language; Love and Lust
- Let Your Body Attract
- Indications of interest from the other.
- Conversation openers.
- Power of the touch.

Conclusion..251
About the Author..254
BONUS
A to Z Dictionary of Gestures and Non-verbal Cues
Available for download

Preface

There are many channels of communication and each are valuable, non-verbal communication being one of them. When we gain knowledge of this silent language we can understand that of all communication, non-verbal language holds a higher importance above the rest, as it is the largest way we present to others. We are all expressing non-verbal communication, yet we hardly notice that we are doing it; and this is the most reliable sources of truthful information.

Alchemy amongst other things is also known to be protoscience, a practice aimed to purify, mature, and perfect certain objects. Along with philosophy which actuates existence, knowledge, reason, mind, and language. Alchemy uses Protoscience to unveil truths through evidence, rather than theory and predetermined belief.

When we are fortunate enough to discover truth, and understand obstruction of time, we can put this evidence into practice, truth can and will only take us to a better life experience of joy, comfort and fulfilled desires.

Alchemical practices have been used on us from the moment of birth and during our early development we were influenced with conditioned reasoning, beliefs and language. These verbal and non-verbal programs which are usually taught to us with good intention, have been stored in our subconscious mind to involuntary drive our present expressions, attitudes, and more importantly our life results. Regardless of the intended goodness, those in our overall environment expressed and taught without realising the extent of what they were doing and therefore left us to feel unwanted emotions along with unfulfilled goals, goals that seem out of our reach.

Actions speak louder than words and non-verbal language is the literal connection to this statement. Non- verbal language also known as body language is available to us inherently and naturally. It comes spontaneously and without effort. All we need do is to know how to decode, interpret and develop this inherent skill to its fullest potential.

What you will learn from this book will be beneficial to you in every activity you engage in. Use this book as a reference to aid others, but more importantly for yourself. Use the knowledge to unveil your subconscious blocks, or the conditioned beliefs that interfere with attaining a life you desire. A better life experience awaits you.

Introduction

Gaze in non-verbal communication can differ in strength and frequency. An affectionate parent kneels and brings eyes to level with the child, whereas, those that are less affectionate lean forward and use gaze less frequently. These experiences from our early development, (our childhood) have formulated our patterns which present as automatic, involuntary body language. Only with conscious effort can we change them, but first, we must understand the purpose and function of gaze as well as our body language to discover what habits really are.

Verbal communication is considered to be the foremost means of communicating, however, extensive research carried out by *Professor Albert Mehrabian* at the University of California, Los Angeles, has proven that through the mouth, voice communication is just a fraction of expression and communication. Words account to only 7% of the overall way we convey a message. Tone of voice (sound) accounts for 38%, and the highest, **body language, accounts for 55%** of our expression and communication.

Body language is the oldest and most powerful means of communication, yet, though it has the highest percentage for communication delivery, it is very much neglected and misunderstood. By learning this knowledge, you get to see what other people cannot. Its like x-ray vision to secret thoughts, even a way to discover hidden suppresions within yourself, such as; what is holding you back and why you have unwanted results in your life. This knowledge and practice of mindful, responsive communication can magically manifest great results into our lives especially when we clear involuntary response templates and replace them with ones that serve us well.

During one basketball game a sports commentator stated, *"Air Jordan used a little **Body English** to coax that ball into the hoop as he released the free throw."* What he meant by this is that the player, Michael Jordan, moved his hips sideways, as if using mind control, so that the ball will go through the basket. And it did.

Body English is a powerful process we can learn to apply in order to bring desired results in a life. Body English whether consciously or unconsciously is just one of the multiple of examples of body language that we do anyway. When we learn to harness the power of this and use it consciously we can make magic happen.

By understanding body language, you will be able to decode hidden emotions. You can even decipher if a person is telling the truth or not. Moreover, you can apply body language techniques to convey your intentions to other people. This will ultimately lead you to success in fruitful relationships, at work, socially and the greatest of all, knowing your own hidden, suppressed thoughts and feelings.

The following pages show how to efficiently decode movements and gestures of others, and more importantly, to unveil your own inner emotions and patterns of unconscious body language that blocks your path to successes.

You will learn how how to recognise various cues and emotions such as nervousness, openness, anger, boredom, doubt, frustration, or excitement simply by observing gestures, facial expressions, and postures. As well as gain understanding in the nature of the subconscious mind.

You can use the knowledge to identify if confidence, dominance, and other characteristics are inherent in people. On the contrary, you may also perform these gestures when you want to convey certain traits to subconsciously attain your desired results.

You will learn to interpret certain actions and adapt to any situation. Communicating with others will be a much easier task, you will have a better understanding of the templates that spontaneously create automatic body language and have a clear understanding about your automatic, unconscious imprints. .

Once knowledge has been gained you can use this knowledge to succeed in advancing your life experience. Body language is an eye opener. This golden knowledge will give you clarity, motion you away from confusion and darkness, and it is very easy to learn. Soon you can be expressing body movements to achieve the success you have longed for.

Chapter 1
What is Body Language?

Body language is the unspoken or non-verbal mode of communication that we do in every single aspect of our interaction with others. It is the message board that tells us what the other person thinks and feels in response to our words or actions, as well as responses to their hidden inner thoughts and feelings. Body language involves gestures, mannerisms, and other bodily signs. These non-verbal signals make up a vast part of daily communication from facial expressions to body movements, and it is the things we or others don't say that convey the greatest volumes of information.

Historically verbal communication evolved long after non-verbal communication which is a bonus for us because primordial non-verbal language is deeply rooted in our subconscious and this is why we naturally use gestures while we talk.

Body language applies throughout many facets of our lives. It aids in personal, intimate and professional relationships, in sales, at work, and even with YOU. Understanding body language is useful in life because regardless of what we do, work, shop or socialise, people will always be part of our life.

Why is Body Language Essential Knowledge?

Verbal Communication is interpreted from our actions and body positions, not just from the words or sound. When people speak, we can tell their emotions by how they bodies express, and how they use their hands, which words they emphasise, and where they pause in speech. As stated previously verbal communication accounts for only seven percent of all the messages that we convey. Unlike body language which accounts for fifty five percent of our communication. This shows us how important our body language is for communication and for achieving results.

Our ability to use body language in a positive way and to read other people's minds through their body language is a powerful craft to our overall personal development and life results. Understanding body language can advance us in becoming proficient at both reading, delivering non-verbal messages and getting the results we want.

Imagine creating a great impression for business, and relationships through the knowledge of this not-so-practiced yet powerful field of study. Imagine being in total control of your own outcomes. Well, YOU CAN! You perform the magic for non-verbal incantations, YOU are the alchemist. It is the unspoken tool to a successful life and more still you can use the power of prediction to choose your next steps, especially when you know what hidden foundations are, and how non-verbal communication affects and **infects** us through the mastermind in ways most are oblivious to.

The Mastermind and Incantation

When two or more minds come together a mastermind is created. Napoleon Hill in his book, *Think and grow Rich*, wrote, *"No two minds ever come together without thereby creating a third, invisible intangible force, which may be likened to a third mind [the master mind]."*

When we interact with others our subconscious mind absorbs all communication around us. This includes speech, sound (tone of voice) and the biggest of all non-verbal patterns. Extensive research has shown that our subconscious mirrors the non-verbal patterns of others. These patterns are the hidden thoughts and emotions that involuntarily and automatically express in body gestures. Like magic, our minds connect without us knowing, we feed one another and begin to express the mannerisms of those that dominate the interaction. This connection is what Napoleon refers to as, *"a third, invisible intangible force"*

Whether we are communicating with one other or many, this *third mind, the intangible force* is created. This is why by association people have similar; illnesses, speech patterns, problems, joys as well as financial situations. We become the other by default through the subconscious mind. For example;
A group of friends begin to use a similar language such as slang, speaking with a nasal tone, dress sense and body posture. Another is a shared stress due to not enough money to cover the bills, working hard for the money and money comes in, yet goes out even quicker. The concerns of another, particularly the transmission of emotion, is absorbed into our limbic brain system and transmuted to become our own emotion; this in turn becomes our new third mind, ready to give us the same results.

It raises the importance of who do you associate with, more so than who do you listen to. Body language expresses the hidden, silent language and even if a person appears to be happy such as singing or verbally communicating about all the great things in their life, this may not be the truth. The mouth can lie, **the body cannot.** Who do you interact with often and what are your results?

Science and Quantum physics has proven that everything has a cause, and this creates an affect. Every verbal sound and non-verbal expression during interaction creates the affect (outcome), and the cause is likened to an incantation. Magic spells or charms performed through a series of verbal and silent words (gestures). All our communication operates as incantations to us and to others. The through the mouth words and body expressions enchant immediately and throughout interaction; and attach to the subconscious mind to create the *third mind*.

Energy Inoculation

Have you ever wondered what it would be like to see into the minds of other?

Let's say you asked someone to do a task. They agree to do it, however, somehow you know, perhaps your intuition is saying they don't really want to do it, regardless of them saying yes. You can question them directly, however, their verbal reply may not be indicative of what they really think or feel.

You can never determine the truthfulness or sincerity of people by what they say alone. In fact, words transmitted verbally oftentimes do not reflect what people really think or feel.

When we communicate with others, we assume we only respond to what is being said, heard or generally seen. There is so much more involved and most of us do not pick up on the body language of others, especially our own. Body language gives us an impression of others and an expression of ourselves. It shows hidden emotions and provides valuable information for true thoughts and feelings.

We have habits that are instilled and we received these through our environments; there where and who we grew up with. These habits are courtesy, not wanting to make waves, cause inconvenience, displease or concern others that we often withhold our true thoughts and feelings. Instead we conform to the status quo of what polite behaviour is and compromise ourselves. This is known as hidden thoughts, and regardless of our good intentions, oftentimes we are not in complete awareness of our unconscious competant behaviour.

Imagine a large syringe, and in this is an energy serum called beliefs, preferred practice and cloning. When interacting with others this serum is created from their words, physical mannerisms, beliefs and emotions. Everything they say and do fills up the syringe and we without choice are innoculted with this, only this injection is applied to the brain rather than the arm. We now have cloned patterns and instilled habits, and these become our hidden thoughts.

These hidden thoughts automatically and involuntarily action our body movements and gestures; and these actions when understood, provide a treasure trove of information that can be used in creating successful outcomes.

The ultimate solution to knowing truthfulness, sincerity and many other circumstances is to read body movements and gestures. This way you can determine the true inner works of others, including yourself because… **The Body Never Lies!**

Automatic Body Language

Knowledge of body language is important; however, it is also essential to understand and pay attention to other cues such as context. It is beneficial to observe the signals, movements and gestures, as a group rather than focusing on a single action. This can reveal inner works; subconscious thoughts and patterns that physically express involuntarily and automatically.

These automatic responses are ones that most people are unaware of. They are unconscious competent responses (reactions). Feedback that comes from the subconscious mind that is projected involuntarily and performed naturally without concentration, and usually without realisation.

These responses are aspects of ourselves and our experiences we don't like to admit exist, even traits we are oblivious to, yet, they come out regardless of our attempt to hide them. This is known as projection. And until we are able to recognise this, we will continue the endless cycles of projection and reaction. The famous Swiss psychiatrist and psychoanalyst Carl Jung stated, *"A man who is unconscious of himself acts in a blind, instinctive way and is in addition fooled by all the illusions that arise when he sees everything that he is not conscious of in himself coming to meet him from outside as projections upon his neighbour."*

Often, our gestures are fluid and subconscious. We tilt our heads in question, use our hands to punctuate a point, cross our arms to ward off discomfort or cross our legs with toes pointing upward for protection, all without realising how and why we are moving or expressing these ways. Automatic body language is something that afflicts us all to varying degrees due to personality, individual differences and the most common of all; automatic responses that are our hidden aspects. Our fears and experiences from the past, especially from childhood.

When we start to observe automatic body language in ourselves and others it sheds light on how we view ourself, why we have certain results in our life and what barriers stop us from moving forward to better life experiences. These observations teach us a lot about our automatic habits and the automatic habits of others. These habits are templates, patterns that guide our physical form. These templates have been stored in our subconscious, and are our life obstacles of unworthyness, disappointment, fear and failure.

Our deep seeded emotions are part and parcel of these templates. Our hidden emotions along with our hidden obstacles will present as our external physical expressions, and we, the individual are unconscious of these projections. Often, we and others project inconsistent messages of feelings and attitudes that during communication are misquoted and misinterpreted. The unsuspecting behaviour of these unconscious reactions are the result of miscommunication. The why. Why some seem to misquote and misinterpret communication, therefore having inaccurate judgements.

Our mind will continue to respond with automatic body language and gestures that match subconscious imprints. The imprints also apply to our verbal conversation. These are our speech patterns and responses such as; how are you? (Automatic question). Good (automatic response). Our subconscious mind projects patterns for us continually and in various circumstances. Here are some examples:

Visually:

"Don't think of a black horse with a red saddle" your mind automatically images a black horse.

Inner beliefs:

In a job interview: "Tell me about yourself". Your mind brings to the surface the subconscious imprints and these present in the body language such as nervousness due to a deep seeded belief of unworthiness, disappointment or failure.

The great news is that you CAN change automatic body language. This first step is recognition. When we are aware of something is has less power over us. Here are some ways to assist you in changing, even stopping your automatic body language:

- Tune in and observe your body's conversational movements and once you have noticed these patterns you can consciously master your own body language as well as giving yourself the opportunity to let go of the imprints that don't give you the results that you want.

- Practice in the mirror. This can reveal how your body language expresses. By watching your reflection you can pick up on automatic language. Particularly your facial gestures. Talk to yourself, such as; "Look how happy you are" or "you're super smart and popular". Does your subconscious mind believe you? Watch what your hidden thoughts signal. Do your eyes look away, this indicates discomfort. Are you blinking more, this indicates inner struggle. Are you exhaling this indicates easing the discomfort. What are your eyebrows, mouth, even feet and hands doing? These too can signal what your true feelings are.

- The best way to discover your automatic body language is to watch a video recording of yourself. Watch your body language and gestures. See if they match the words you are saying in this video. This is very much an eye opener for anyone and you get to see what others see. It can be quite confronting, but don't let this stop you. Move forward in observing yourself in order to deal with and alter these projections once they are discovered.

- Another way is to listen to, not ask, what others say to you, about you. These patterns are seen by others and you may find clues to your unrecognised habits.

Remember this... Any imprint was instilled at a previous time, the past. The past is nothing but ether, blank air now. It's only the memories we give power to that keep interfering in our path to success. This now non-existent past has no place in giving you the results you desire. This is impossible, because you are not that child or teenager any longer. Nor are you that employee, partner or title of former experiences. You live in a place called here, right NOW and every NOW is a new phase of your life for you to choose and create very different memories.

Practice, observe and apply the knowledge you have gained. A better life experience awaits you. You are the Alchemist.

"In any given moment we're guided by one of two maps — a vision map, which is a deliberate plan for our future, or a default map, which is made up of our past. The quickest way out of pain is through it, it's only when we have the courage to face things exactly as they are without any self-deception or illusion that a light can develop by which the path to success will be recognized." - Debbie Ford

Chapter 2
Fundamentals of body language

Reading outer expressions is quite simple once the language is learned. At first it may seem difficult to remember all the cues, but with practice this second language will flow naturally and quite often, very quickly.

Body language is fluid and occurs around us all the time. Many can observe some of the cues just through common sense, however, it is important not to look at signals one by one. Instead we should piece together all the cues to establish the full meaning. This means non-verbal signals in relation to verbal communication must be considered, as well as the situation as a whole. Otherwise, only a portion of the story is read rather than all the chapters that gives clarity in understanding the whole story.

Learning more about how to improve your own non-verbal expression as well as your whole story will aid in better communication of your wants and feelings. This results in achievement of your desired outcomes, and you can do this without even saying a word. It also greatly increases your life to exceptional because as you now know you can learn more about yourself and interrupt the unconscious competent automatic responses (reactions) of your own body language.

With knowledge of body language, you accomplish better communication with others and gain insight in interpreting what others might be trying to convey, as well as recognising their unconscious imprints. Body movement and gestures helps us predict the emotions and thoughts of people around us. It also gives us the foundations and framework to understand them. It's like having psychic abilities.

The Fortune Teller

We all already have some sort of intuitive ability to read people much like a fortune teller, we simply require the knowledge of body and gesture signals.

Fundamentally, body language is an involuntary and unconscious response, otherwise known as automatic body language. Fortune tellers are proficient at intuitively reading body language, and a part of telling fortunes can rely upon the individual's signals, more so the involuntary, automatic responses. Tellers are able to notice subtle body language cues and by these they can navigate the reading. These cues are small gestures such as; altered breathing, posture signals and facial expressions; and these clues can indicate if the reading is going in the right or wrong direction. Here's another example:

When deep desires are mentioned tension can project in the physical body and this is another signal where the reader can aid in giving comfort to the customer.

Knowing body language is helpful in numerous ways, not just in the telling of fortunes. Here are some useful examples:

As a public speaker you can pick up on audience signals. They may be uninterested, overwhelmed, arms crossed, leg crossed, or both. This indicates that it's time to switch tactics or to get the audience involved. Alternatively, they may present a head tilt, which indicates your presentation is right on track.

As a parent, body language will assist in understanding your children, even in understanding your partner/husband/wife. There's no need to read minds to discover the hidden emotions of your loved ones, just read their body language.

Mind strings

Mind strings are triggers which when set or "pulled on" by a stimuli create predictable responses in people. A comparison to mind strings is a piano. When keys are pressed, a string is pulled creating a predictable result, a sound.

The mind, through suggestion and daily life, works similar to the piano. When certain triggers are hit, a person will output predictable responses. For example, when a person is suddenly yelled at, they react with surprise or are startled, or when presented with images of salty chips, they begin to salivate. All people are collections of their past including what was created through evolution, and it is this conditioned foundation that produces strings which can be pulled. Mind strings are valuable in body language as they can be pulled to create desirable results. For example, many people have a mind string which says that celebrities are worthy of attention and those who are street vagrants, are not. Mind strings are the habitual beliefs held by the majority and past down from generations. They are automatic suggestions, or involuntary hypnosis, that has been absorbed but our subconscious mind because we listened, observed, and mimicked the people around us. Because of this we already have many mind strings, therefore we can relate to others because we know their habitual triggers. Much like a mind reader we can predict the outcomes or take part in altering them.

First Impressions

You may have heard the statement "Don't judge a book by its cover." Yet human nature still judges what people are wearing, how clean and tidy they are, or by obvious physical traits. First impressions are much like these judgements. They hold strength in judgement, and often another's first impression of us does not match how we view ourselves, nor does our initial impression match that of another. So why is it that we don't see eye to eye?

A small portion of initial impressions are determined by what we say verbally, the larger portion is from our non-verbal signals, and the result is decided in the first four minutes.

Once a judgment has been determined, many people resist in changing their opinion, and due to automatic body language, hidden emotional impressions are expressed passively, and involuntarily, regardless of our desire to be seen in a positive light. Therefore, it is important that we know this and learn how to use it as an advantage rather than by default.

By consciously assessing any meeting, whether personal or professional we can instantly read the body language cues. With this knowledge we can stay on alert of our own body language and deliberately emphasise relevant impressions to suit the individual/s preferences. After the four minutes, we can relax back to our natural selves and allow the now decided positive opinion to flow in the conversation.

Reading People

Reading body language comprises of all the signals, both verbal and nonverbal, knowing what is irrelevant and connecting only the relevant to decode the meaning. The whole picture should be determined when all or most of the factors are connected. Therefore, paying attention to all communication expressions during any get together gives us more clues as to what is really going on. It also gives us opportunity to observe contradictions between what someone is saying and their body language. Here an example;

Someone may be telling the truth of a situation, yet they fidget, avoid eye contact and touch their nose. Though what they are saying may be true, these conflicting signals indicate uncertainty (not lying) with the information being verbalised. Another possibility is that this person is fatigued or suffers from a neuro medical condition. As you can see, paying attention to all the cues matters because of other possibilities that may be involved.

Why the Body Never Lies

Our amygdala is a part of the brain that is the distributor of our emotions. It decodes the information received from our inner senses (feelings) then initiates the format of body function. It then sends this format through internal connections to arrive at the motor system known as our body.

The limbic system, a set of brain centres that include the amygdala, hippocampus, anterior thalamic nuclei, and limbic cortex control emotion, behaviour, long term memory and the sense of smell. Together they react to the stimulus of the world around us and are responsible for our non-verbal response. The limbic brain controls emotional body language, the true honest response of our inner workings, and is our guide to indicate what the body is really feeling. It is the limbic brain that controls the arms, feet, hands, heads, and body when someone is feeling happy, sad, embarrassed, ashamed, afraid or excited, and so on.

The limbic brain also tells us when to be scared and what to do about it, whether it's to fidget, freeze up or to run. It tells us which way to point our feet such as up for protection, to move and jump with joy or to jitter and point a foot towards an exit in preparation to leave when bored.

When someone is lying they may be able to control the words, however, they cannot control their automatic body reactions to these words, nor can they control their gestures and facial expressions, because the limbic system has already created the external responses based on the hidden inner feelings. Telling a lie is difficult when holding honest gestures, such as palms exposed, because the brain system already knows your discomfort about being untruthful and acts to express the body accordingly. Just as when someone is dancing, it is difficult to have a negative attitude because the format can only present as emotions connected to dancing. This is why and how we can observe cues during lies, because the body language presents as fear, stress, sadness, anger and so on.

Regardless of what we try to pretend on the outside, our brain will always tell the body what to do based on the inner emotions. Body language, for this reason, is very powerful. When we understand gestures related to opened and closed minds (this will be explained in a later chapter), we can create positive changes in ourselves that will improve our life experiences. We can even aid others in emotional changes by the use of mirroring, this too will be explained later on.

Observe Signals as a Group

Always observe non-verbal signals in relation to verbal communication and consider the situation as a whole for clarity in understanding. A single gesture can mean any number of things, or maybe even nothing at all. The key to accurately reading non-verbal behaviour is to look for groups of signals that reinforce a common point. If you place too much emphasis on just one signal out of many, you might come to an inaccurate conclusion about what a person is communicating.

Consider Context

You may have heard others remark about verbal statements that are taken out of context. This applies to non-verbal language as well.

When you are communicating with others, always consider the situation and the context in which the communication occurs. Concluding that someone is rude or ignorant from a single cue is an example of ignoring context. Temperature can affect cues such as; someone who crosses their arms could be defined as closed or protective, yet they may also be cold. Alternatively, removing a jacket could mean that a person is warming up to others, yet, it could also mean that they are overheating.

Some situations require formal or structured behaviours that might be interpreted differently in any other setting such as; the body language expressed at work can be very different from the signals we would express in a family get together. Consider whether or not non-verbal behaviours are appropriate for the context. If you are trying to improve your own non-verbal communication, apply practices that enable your signals to match the level of formality or structure presented by the situation. Attune your gestures, speech and voice to the suit the situation, this will blend harmoniously and ensure that you are conveying expressions that others want to see, in such a way that you are in control, this enables you to achieve your choice in results. Because you are playing the game, not being the game.

Understanding Context

The purpose of observing context is to find cues that can be guided towards a more positive direction. When body language expresses negative impressions, context can reveal the cause and this useful information guides us in the process of eliminating unwanted results. Below is a scenario used with examples for Understanding and Applying Context.

You are in a conversation and you notice that your friend has crossed their arms, leaned away from you, and is repeatedly rubbing their face. Why is your friend uncomfortable?

This discomfort can be a result of them not liking the topic of conversation. Or they may be uncomfortable because you have food stuck to your tooth and they're not sure if they should tell you. Another reason could be that something is wrong and has nothing to do with you, such as an upset stomach.

If you only look at their body language, you won't have enough information to identify the source of their discomfort. Body language will tell you that someone is comfortable or uncomfortable, and with only one signal the why is not always so clear. This is why you look at the context. Considering context means to be observant of three aspects:

The conversation - Did something in the conversation trigger your friend to become more comfortable or uncomfortable? If your friend's language changed when you asked a specific question, perhaps there is something about that question that made them uncomfortable.

The environment - Observe the room you both are in to see what may have caused the reaction. Perhaps an argument at a nearby table, an influx of customers now making the room crowded, an ex-partner may have entered or a number of other possibilities to prompt this discomfort.

Recent experiences - An occurrence your friend had prior to your conversation may be affecting them. For example; a rough day at work or an unexpected expense. These discomfort signals may be the result of them still thinking about the stressful day.

Applying Context

Once you have identified potential causes for your friend's discomfort aid in eliminating the unease if you can and see if your friend becomes comfortable. Let's say their body language signalled discomfort when you spoke about a controversial topic. Change the topic and see if their body language relaxes. If it is something close by, such as a person, suggest relocating to another table or even another venue, and observe their response. If you cannot conclude the source of their discomfort, ask them what's wrong. Even if you don't know the source of their discomfort, you can still help in easing them. It's preferable to know the specific source of their distress, but simply being aware that they are uncomfortable goes a long way.

Considering context can seem overwhelming at first due to looking at the conditions as well as focusing upon the conversation. However, through practice you will find this becomes a very simple and natural process.

Four Keystones

Single gestures alone do not reveal the true meaning of any situation. These are only portions of the story. To gain clarity in understanding the whole story, more factors come into reading body language, particularly, because when people move, they are fluid and changing, so too are their moods and context. This is where the 'four keystones' are helpful; context, comparison, intuition and something that is in accordance with another.

These keystones help us to read cues alongside other cues before drawing conclusions. This is known as bundling. The more cues that associate and co-work to other cues, the more accurate we can be in unveiling the underlying meaning. Here are some examples of bundling;

- When a person is sitting with arms tightly pressed against the chest, this can mean they are uncomfortable, yet, it can also mean that a person is cold. Scratching the nose or face can mean that a person is lying or it could simply be an itch. However, touching the nose, wiping the mouth in a down-stroke, avoiding eye contact and fidgeting tells us that a downright lie is being expressed.

- Crossing the legs by bringing one foot over the opposite leg, the fingers are interlinked together, body leaning back in the chair, the head tilting back, and looking down through the nose at others. This reveals arrogance and superiority. However, a mild crotch display on its own, means very little.

- Arms crossed tightly over the chest, legs crossed, head down and shoulders pulled inward. This shows discomfort and closing off the outside world.

This does not mean that we should not read body language with only one or two cues. One or two cues is sometimes all that is expressed. However, applying bundling when possible aids in the whole story conclusion, along with deeper hidden stories.

The Dishonest and Honest Body

Facial expressions can appear genuine and honest, they show concern, fear, disgust, or happiness, however, bodies do not always reflect these. The body can express mixed messages. People often wear a mask, not always just one, there can be multiple masks.

At an early age we paid attention to facial expressions and this became a way we in which we learned to control the face by mimicking these expressions, this also became mind string patterns. Therefore, this mimic routine can make the face an unreliable source when we are determining signals because it is dishonest body language.

Dishonest body language reveals a lot about true thoughts and feelings. Environment (society) requires us to act in certain ways, regardless of difficulty, hardship or sorrow we may be experiencing. We are told to stay strong, which fundamentally means to suppress our true emotions. We have heard statements such as; "Turn that frown upside down", "Wipe that look off your face" and "Smile for the camera" We have even been taught to suppress our thoughts and become manipulators by begging. For example: "What's the magic word" A child is prompted to say "please", even though they don't really mean it. And they learn quite quickly that this form of needy manipulation gets results. To make matters worse, we have been taught that this word is a form of manners, and manners are supposedly good, regardless of our true intention. There is one thing right about this though. The word is a composition of three syllables, man-n-ers. Originally meaning; man (person) - n (noun for people) - ers (abbreviation of errors). The original meaning for error is; a deviation from truth, wrong-doing, or sin. Therefore, when we (people/man) say please, and don't mean it, good manners indicate that we are being good, sinful liars… hmmm.

Along with suppressing or lying about what we truly think, we also mask negative body language to avoid appearing rude, insensitive, weak, and afraid, or purely to conceal that we may feel disadvantaged in a situation.

If someone is bored during an interaction they will still nod and smile during the conversation, yet their body will orientate in the direction of the doorway, and they will also glance a few times at a clock or watch. Happiness expressions mixed with cues such as gripping the arms or hands tightly is a signal that indicates the reverse. A person is unhappy and stressed. A person who leans forward enthusiastically and acts pleased to offer a hand shake; and their jaw clenches tightly whilst verbally greeting you, indicates they have some negative issues with you and they are unhappy to be in your presence.

Eventually, we get very good at masking negative emotions through our facial expressions, we play the game of pretend. We pretend to be interested, nice, happy or pleased. However, it doesn't matter how we choose to impersonate, the subconscious mind will always express truth of our inner feelings; and relay it through other parts of the body.

Negative body language is automatic, it occurs because we don't want people to know that we are upset, scared, bored, shy or bothered in some way. The limbic brain as mentioned earlier has already created the response for our true emotions. If we are thinking or feeling it, it will definitely project in external expression.

The opposite of dishonest, and pretend body language are the expressions that indicate true honest feelings. Honest cues happen quickly, sometimes as micro expressions that can reveal something predictive such as; a twitch of the muscles between the eyes, (the fear muscle). This cue shows the eyebrows forming a grin-like gesture that reveals a fear-based thought.

So how do we detect honest signals emanating from various parts of the body?

By the feet! Feet are excellent predictors about what our minds and bodies wish to do. Just as a finger points to signal attention to something or someone, so too, can the feet. However, with feet the signal is leaked by accident, rather than for attention.

Feet are the utmost reliable source for the display of truth. Feet can conflict with messages expressed by the face, arms, hands and legs? However, though this is a great source for cues we should always observe other non-verbal body language first such as; the face, arms, hands, legs, feet, and torso.

Through evolution our hands became useful to carry out tasks, we learned to occupy them with tasks such as; building, drawing and throwing. Our feet, however, were left to carry out traditional tasks like escaping predators or avoiding sharp and hot surfaces. When we are frightened or startled our automatic body language can be feet tucked under our legs and coiled up, freezing instantly, or we pull them up onto a chair because a mouse has scurried across a room. The feet are the initial responders for fight or flight action.

Our feet lead us even while seated, they reveal the direction we plan to go or explore once the right circumstances or opportunity presents itself. When someone is interested in another their feet will leak out this desire. Lack in interest is shown as; in a seated position, hips swivel towards another yet feet are facing away. This orientation indicates politeness, the hips swivel only to face the speaker. However, feet oriented toward another, indicates interest, or attraction.

Feet reveal positive and negative cues. Here are some examples;

When children are interested in play rather than another task, such as eating, their legs bounce, or their feet will point toward the direction of their play area, ready for escape. They quickly eat their meal, so they can return to play.

When held by a parent that has been absent for a short while, such as work. A baby or toddler will kick up and down, and the entire body will jump with joy regardless of a confined embrace.

Jittery feet, including legs expresses fidgeting and indicates boredom. Jittery can also be due to nervous energy or the result of happiness (happy feet). Context will aid in concluding the body language of this expression.

Adults reveal true emotions by pointing feet away from boring conversations or when intimately interested in another the feet point toward the object of interest.

In stressful situations such as attending the dentist or doctor, toes point to the exit. The same gesture occurs when someone is not interested in another or wants to end a conversation.

People of all ages can seem to float on air (light on their feet). This gravity defying body language indicates joy and excitement.

Quite often the body language of feet is left unnoticed. They may be tucked under table or hidden under clothing. Our feet and legs display significant cues, some include; protection or defence by pointing the toes upward, boredom through repetitive motions, joy by lifting them up and down, fear by tucking them under a chair, depression by being motionless or sensuality by being uncovered and flaunted. The list goes on.

Observe the feet as much as possible, foot and leg language are cues that indicate true hidden meaning and emotions that is much more reliable than other body language cues.

Chapter 3
Nature of People

Introverts and Extroverts

Fundamentally there are two types of personalities introverted and extroverted

Introverted

A personality that is inward thinking, recharge by seclusion and reflection. They work well independently prefer quiet areas with little distraction. These personalities are in no way antisocial, they simply feel more comfortable in being alone with their own thoughts rather than in the spotlight.

Body language- introverts in public places or circumstances with too much activity will be rigid and they zone out more quickly. They look for quiet places and are often the ones at ease being alone when at a social gathering. They spend more time at home and less on outings. Their non-verbal language expresses more closed body positions; shoulders will pull in, body oriented away from others, there is less eye contact, they may be less animated, are soft spoken, and will often be the ones speaking less, so that they may listen or observe others instead.

Communicating- Meet in quiet areas with little distraction, keep groups as small as possible. One on one is the best scenario for an introvert. Speak quietly, reduce eye contact, and avoid touch.

Extroverted-

A personality that enjoys social situations, these social gatherings to them are stimulating. They are comfortable at busy places such as; shopping centres or cities. They enjoy attention and the spotlight.

Body language- Extroverts spontaneously turn toward people. They interact with random people, touch more in conversation and talk more frequently to keep the conversation going. They use more gestures, move about a room more, and jump from person to person in order to gain more stimulation.

Communicating- Be energetic, speak louder with more expressions, touch often, move in closer, and connect with eye contact.

These personality types respond to how their wired brain processes. A quick way to establish introversion from extroversion is to observe how people break their gaze. Introverts will break their gaze by looking to the right, whereas extroverts will look to the left.

Arm crossing, or tucking hands in pockets, are ways to raise barriers when uncomfortable. These postures are not always negative, they simply indicate that someone needs more time to adjust to new people. Introverts will be found to hold this posture more frequently and longer than extroverts. Extroverts can warm up to people quickly that timidity does not present at all and feel at home with many groups. When dealing with an introvert, offering a drink gives their hands something to do and aids to break their rigidity. Providing an environment where your ideas are accepted, first begins with removing barriers, especially the non-verbal ones.

Body Language and Age

Babies communicate through non-verbal channels by using postures and gestures, and if this does not work they will resort to crying. It is their body language which helps us to figure out their true desires. But what of other age groups that do not use only body language?

As children age, they still rely, as adults do, on non-verbal language such as; pointing at a toy rather than asking for it, pushing other children aside when they want to attain something, frowning to gain sympathy or even hug to show affection.

Children are not skilled at lying through verbal communication and often slip up revealing inconsistencies in their stories. When a child is being untruthful they often avoid eye contact or; they might hang their head, appear tense, they may even quickly cover their mouth to cover the lie, they can also use slouching and pouting to show that they are upset and disappointed. Even adults can express these cues if they slip out a secret or gossip in the wrong circle. As we get older these responses slowly become a touch to the corner of the mouth and later, become a touch to the side of the nose instead.

People that are closest to our age are the easiest to read. This is due to our instinctive ability to relate and empathise during certain stages of growth. For example; siblings of a similar age, have an uncanny ability to interpret and understand each other, much like small children who understand each other's babble and random movements. The greater the gap in age, the more we need to observe for accuracy.

Older faces have weaker muscle tone, therefore they produce less expression and many expressions are disguised by wrinkles. Eyes can relay cues such as a sparkle or blandness however, empathising with seniors by putting yourself in their position, and seeing the world as they do will greatly assist.

Our ability to empathise with the needs, desires and emotions of others is a key part in reading body language. Empathy is the ability to put ourselves in the shoes of others and to feel what they feel.

Grooming

Anything done to maintain our physical appearance is considered grooming such as; brushing our hair, washing our bodies, wearing clean and coordinated clothing, brushing our teeth and so on. Grooming communicates that we are healthy and in a good state of mind.

Mental health has been linked to grooming. When someone is mentally ill it has been noted that physical maintenance is neglected. When a mind is occupied with more pressing matters it does not consider looking good and fresh as a priority. People who are severely depressed will present with unkempt hair, dirty clothing and may have unpleasant odour due to lack in showering. They can be lethargic, their posture will be slumped, shoulders rolled inward, torsos bent at the waste and their head will droop as if the weight of the world sits upon their shoulders.

In opposite to this people that are cheerful express a bounce in their step and present as clean, refreshed and tidy. This is why it is important to keep a well-cared for appearance so that we signal to others that we have stable mental health.

A lot can be derived about a person who is wearing torn and soiled clothing, especially in public. Like attitudes, grooming tells others that we respect their thoughts and opinions, and that we wish to belong to a functioning society.

Grooming is a good, examples can be; adjusting a necktie, tidying the hair, smoothing clothing or applying lipstick (in a date setting, indicates interest and a desire to impress). However, there are some mannerisms with grooming that can be seen as rude such as; picking lint to detach oneself from a conversation and removing dirt from under the nails or clipping them in public. When grooming is performed on someone else, it shows a desire to be close. This is expressed when a parent cleans the dirty hands of their child and when a lover wipes food from their partner's mouth.

Clothing

Our fashion choice is vital information and is a language onto itself. Even prior to speaking with one another our clothing formulates an image about us, it indicates our sex, age, occupation, origins, social class, personality and beliefs.

As an expressive language clothing can be conventional or eccentric and expresses signals about who one wants to be or become. Clothing can express where we are going as well as what we are about to do, for example; A business suit can indicate that one is portraying professionalism, or a t-shirt and shorts can indicate leisure. In other words, clothing provides context.

Clothes can be selected to impress or fit in, and reasons for this can be to avoid embarrassment, discrimination or judgement. Clothing can also be selected to express, set us apart from others in terms of values and the eccentric often have flamboyant clothing to stand out from the rest and to show that their ideas about life are different. These expressions can also include piercings, tattoos, chains and dirty worn clothing

How clothing is fitted also indicates frame of mind. For example, an uptight person buttons his collar to the top, a laid back one has a loose tie or does not wear one. Not ironing clothes, dirty shoes or even wearing no shoes, provide details of negative emotions. Loose or tight-fitting clothing can indicate the nature or intention of the person. Removing a tie under a strict dress code indicates that the person is rebellious and defiant. Unbuttoning a blouse to show more cleavage indicates seduction or power play. Even if the boss is wearing casual clothing, this can be power-play indicating that they set the rules and not the employees. Dressing against the grain indicates, I make my own rules.

Clothing plays a big part in first and daily impressions and provides excellent cues for context, however, be mindful of the non-verbal cues you express with respect to dress expression and also those that are given off by others. After all we do have predetermined opinions about what others wear.

Virtual Reality

Automatic body language is so ingrained in us that we even express it in a virtual world.

Online, people create personalised characters or personas to interact with others in a fundamentally rule-free environment. There are no set parameters of ways to interact through the World Wide Web, yet studies have shown that users still portray their automatic non-verbal language. For example: In interactive online games male characters hold larger distances between other males, females move into closer proximity with males and other females. Males also maintain less eye contact with other males whereas females do not.

Another example is our responses in forums or posts (such as Facebook). Regardless of something that exists virtually most feel driven to react to what others have displayed. Fingers begin to type based on conscious and subconscious emotions. If we were to return weeks later and read some of our own replies, posts, and even the posts from others, we would view some of it differently than that of the time we typed our reactions. This is because our limbic brain alerted the nervous system, and our nervous system controlled our fingers to express the body language for us.

The limbic brain leaves no realm untouched.

Chapter 4
The Basics in Body Language

Mastery is achieved when foundations are well in place, therefore the basics are essential for successful body language reading. In the previous chapter of Fundamentals, the 'four keystones' were mentioned; context, comparison, intuition and something that is in accordance with another. Successful reading requires genuine and true conclusions, and this is done by observing the rhythm and flow of body expressions.

Body language is a greater deal more reliable than oral communication because most people do not pay attention to their outward expressions, and many a times their body language and spoken language contradict one another, this is why we should rely heavily on what is happening non-verbally.

Observe Incongruent Behaviours

Pay careful attention to words that do not match non-verbal behaviours.

Our involuntary and automatic body language patterns are often incompatible and contradictory to our verbal speech, this is what it means to be incongruent. Remember, we pick up on fifty five percent of body language, as does the listener when we are talking. These conflicting messages can confound or irritate a listener as they do not know which message to accept; and it opens possibility for false judgement. For example, someone may say they are happy yet their face expresses wrinkles between the brow, and they are staring at the ground, this indicates worry.

Research has shown that when words fail to match up with non-verbal signals, people tend to ignore what has been said and focus instead on non-verbal expressions including moods, thoughts, and emotions. Therefore, if you say something but your body language suggests differently, you now know that your words are wasted energy. It is useful to pay attention to your own non-verbal cues in relation to your words, or just be honest and share your true thoughts.

Get Your Desired Results

Express Confidence;

Confident people move freely without hesitation, make appropriate gestures, and smile often. A confident posture presents as; the shoulders back and upright, the head up and level, and a well-balanced body.

A large part of a person's body language is in direct connection to how life has treated them, and how they treat life in return. All of us experience some hardship, distress, or sorrow in our life, yet some know how to take control and successfully deal with the outcome. Confident body language shows that a person actively takes control of their unpleasant situations, they also seek out better solutions to improve any adversity that comes into their life.

Those who lack confidence are expressing out of habitual and routine behaviour. They walk with a hunched back, are careless with their arm gestures, their face shows a sulk and frown, they often appear sad or tired and their head will droop. Frown lines can be noticeable on their face, however, this is dependent on the length of time they have been this way for permanent wrinkles to produce. They are often unpleasant to be around, have needy attitudes, express false identities by attempting to mimic others and tend to bring others around them down. This body language shows that they allow life to push them around.

When we meet someone, who is not so great, we can subconsciously feel uneasy or suspicious. Sometimes people put on a good temporary act but within a few minutes their bodies relax, the act gradually falters, and their natural automatic expressions reveal the truth.

Have you ever asked others what they see with your outward expressions? Do you portray certain body language that makes you seem pessimistic, timid, weak, rude, superior, unapproachable or negative? Another way is to listen to, not ask, what others say to you... about you. These patterns are seen by others and you may find clues to your unrecognised habits. This feedback is gold in uncovering your unconscious competent behaviour.

Studies have been carried out where people were asked to stand in front of an audience and deliver a speech whilst being recorded. Later these people would watch this video recording and were asked to observe their body language. One person who received negative remarks about her angry face despite believing herself to be a happy and bubbly person, watched her face and bodily expressions reveal resentment and a hard done by attitude. Another who was against people that flaunted themselves in a sexy manner, watched as her body language flirted with the audience.

These examples above indicate the importance of why we should monitor our gestures and facial expressions. When we are consciously aware of our own body language we can alter it to convey the impressions we wish to show to others in order to achieve the results we desire.

As for the two people who watched a video recording of themselves. They are in a fortunate position, and this is because now, they are aware of what impressions they express. They can resolve matters more quickly if they sense negativity or judgement from others. Even with just a small change they could gain rewarding results.

Our bodies automatically leak information without our consent and when we are not experiencing the results we want, we can proactively do something to change it. If others have expressed that you show negative or unpleasant gestures start by doing some of these things; hold your head up high, sit upright, actively listen, smile often despite inner feelings and start acting happy. Experiments have shown that even by forcing a fake smile we can trick our brain into happiness. Our facial expression reflects our inner emotions; however, this same linkage works both ways - we can change our emotional state by altering our facial expression. As an added bonus, it boosts our health by reducing stress and lowering our heart rate.

Body language is a great way to fake it until you make it. Holding confident body language will make you feel confident, so use your body to change the automatic, unconscious patterns and create a new automatic template in your limbic brain system; and watch people around you begin to treat you better.

Body English

The term 'body English' refers to actioning subtle body movements to convey an intended outcome. As if using mind control we can do a physical action whilst thinking of how we choose the outcome to be and the result will play out to our intention. Just as Michael Jordon the basketball player did when he moved his hips sideways so that the ball he threw would curve and go through the basket.

This expression originated around the 1900's in sports such as bowling and ice hockey, where a player would influence the path of a ball or puck by moving their body in a particular direction. It appears to be magic, however, there is a reason for this.

Albert Einstein told us this; *"Everything is energy and that's all there is to it. Match the frequency of the reality you want and you cannot help but get that reality. It can be no other way. This is not philosophy. This is physics."*

"Everything is Energy." This has been proven many times by Nobel Prize winning physicists, such as Niels Bohr, including numerous scientists and quantum physicists from past to present. Things we can see, including us, and that which cannot been seen is energy. And all energy has conscious intent or intention. A purpose, goal and end result.

Body English can be likened to remote intention setting. In the book, *The Intention Experiment by Lynne McTaggart*, numerous scientific studies were performed around the world looking for evidence of intention impacting physical reality. The experiments included prayer, meditation, healing, remote healing, and visualization. Some of these experiments selected people that required healing such as; patients with wounds, children with attention deficit and other medical conditions. These experiments had participating healers across the globe (remotely) set intentions through visualisation, thought and feeling. Results were significant, and patients experienced healing while the intentions were being transmitted, in comparison to times participant healers were 'resting'. This shows us the potential we have to make real change with our thoughts. Remote Intention makes us rethink what happens to our thoughts. It has been proven through the intention experiments, numerous times, that we are connected to everyone and everything.

Thoughts, words, emotions and actions are all energy; and when created carry with it conscious intention to bring into our physical experience the exact match of the frequency we relay.

Michael Jordon, the bowlers and ice hockey players actioned the movements of the balls and pucks, they followed this with conscious intention, they imaged the results in their minds and without doubt knew they controlled the outcome.

Pay Attention to Non-verbal Signals

People can communicate information in numerous ways. Always observe eye contact, gestures, posture, body movements, and tone of voice. All of these signals can convey important information that is not put into words. By paying closer attention to unspoken behaviours, you will improve your own ability to communicate nonverbally.

Tone of Voice

Your tone of voice can convey a wealth of information, ranging from enthusiasm to disinterest to anger. Start noticing how your tone of voice affects others, how they respond to you and try using tone of voice to emphasise ideas that you want to attain or to communicate. For example, if you want to show genuine interest in something, express your enthusiasm by using an animated tone of voice. Remember to consider Introverts and Extroverts. Speak quietly, reduce eye contact, and avoid touch with an introvert. For an extrovert be energetic, speak louder with more expressions, touch often, move in closer, and connect with eye contact.

Eye Contact

When people avoid looking at the eyes of others, this indicates evading or trying to hide something. However, too much eye contact can express as confrontational or intimidating. While eye contact is an important part of communication, it is important to remember that good eye contact does not mean staring fixedly into someone's eyes continually. Eye contact should last for four to five seconds with intervals between. (There is more on eye contact later in the book.)

Ask Questions

If you are unsure of another's non-verbal signals, ask questions for clarity and deeper understanding. You can repeat back what has been said and ask for clarification. An example of this can be, "So what you are saying is that......*Fill in the gap.......*"

Simply asking questions can lend a great deal of transparency to a situation. For example, a person might be expressing certain non-verbal signals such as staring blankly at an object or acting distracted, because their mind is elsewhere. By inquiring further into these cues, you can attain a better idea of what the situation is.

Effective and Meaningful Communication

Remember that verbal and non-verbal communication work together to convey a message with aid of the four keystones; context, comparison, intuition and something that is in accordance with another. You can improve your spoken communication by using body language that reinforces and supports what you are saying. This can be especially useful when making presentations or when speaking to a large group of people. For example, if your goal is to express confidence and of being prepared, during a presentation focus on non-verbal signals that reflect self-assurance and capability. Stand firmly in one place, hold your shoulders back, and balance your weight on both feet.

Signals can be Misread

A firm handshake indicates a strong personality while a weak handshake indicates lack of courage. However, a limp handshake may actually indicate something else entirely, such as arthritis. This example illustrates an important point about the possibility of misreading non-verbal signals. Our conditioned beliefs can have us predetermine another and this can adversely affect the outcome. Always remember to look for groups of expressions rather than a singular gesture. A person's overall body language is far more revealing than a gesture viewed in isolation.

"One must bear courage since by nature are in the habit of labeling, criticizing, giving alibis of justification and finding flaws. Acquiring a mind-set of acceptance assists us in marching on in life without stewing on what was or what could "be – Rhys T. O'Leary, The Only Moment Is Now

Conscious Practice

When in contact with others you can build upon the skill of understanding body language by observing non-verbal behaviour and practicing different types of non-verbal communication with others. Through practice you can vastly improve all your own communication abilities and change your destructive automatic pattern responses.

Intuition and Perception

Often people see what they want to see, instead of what is really occurring. This is preconceived notion and these notions can be misleading. The same pitfalls can arise during the analysis of body language. If we expect to see nervous, angry, happy or confident body language, we will. However, if we do not assume and instead keep an open mind, we may observe something completely different from the initial expectation.

Intuition can be of great assistance in establishing circumstances however, it is important to know when something is intuitive or from memory patterns that preconceive the circumstance. When someone says they feel uneasy or have a bad feeling about someone, they are using their intuition. Sometimes though, our intuition becomes clouded by the preconceived notions and new information is tainted or distorted. This is when reading people can backfire, and it can affect others as well as ourselves negatively.

When observing others always start with clean the slate, see it as a new circumstance in the NOW, and read each cue separately. Many optical illusions or visual tricks rely on the fact that our brains are responsive in finding information we think should be there, rather than looking at information that is actually there.

Most people have not practiced listening to their intuition and are somewhat unsure of what it is, and therefore confusing intuition with assumption or guesstimation. Intuition has been described as the little voice inside our heads and to many this does not make much sense, because not everyone hears the inner voice. Intuition can present in other ways.

Our intuition does not speak to us in words. It speaks to us through dreams, notions, urges, and physical sensations. We have cluttered our thoughts with beliefs and opinions; and when a message comes we miss it, or dismiss it with excuses, interpretations and distractions from external events. Our sensations are our insight, direct or immediate cognition, and our inner guidance. Of all the mental faculties' we possess, intuition is the greater for guidance. It is a thought or sensation which says, "this is the way". A better description for intuition would be 'our spiritual faculty' that is above intellectual understanding. It is a magic path to our inner self and a sense that watches over us and never sleeps. Nothing is irrelevant with intuition because it guides us in the yay or nay of our next step.

We must be attentive to our intuition and give lesser notice to reasoning and perception. Reasoning and perception can be tainted with conditioned beliefs and opinions, and therefore not necessarily be our appropriate guide. Our intellectual understanding has taught us to reason through our beliefs or opinions and sometimes it takes practice to notice only our intuition, rather than perception of circumstances; which is only habits. We have habits; regular habits that are accustomed to doing the same thing every day, such as; waking up and going to bed at a certain time. Any variation, in particular acting on our intuition, can upset our habitual behaviors, however, momentum in practice will overcome these habits that do not ultimately serve us. The practice of tuning into intuition is a must and an important part of development in understanding body language, because this is the straight line and shortest route to confirmation of truth.

Begin to listen to your body. We all have the ability to assess what is right or wrong, what feels good or bad. When you are feeling good this is your inner message or intuition indicating something positive. Take advice from your inner guidance.

Here are some tips for reading your intuition;
An easy way to notice these indications is through sensation. When sensation feels light, warm or tingly, particularly around the chest area, this is our intuition indicating that all is well. If we feel discomfort, a sickly feeling, tension or tightness around the stomach/solar plexus area, our intuition is alerting us about something unpleasant.

However, tuning into your intuition is often not enough. A funny feeling, having a sense or being uneasy about someone or something is of immense value, yet, if you cannot support your intuition with postures and signals such as a poker face (an unassuming, revealing facial expression) this can negatively affect circumstances.

It is wise to practice noticing your intuition, this can aid you in observing others. Every mind is built differently, therefore intuitive responses will differ, however, when we actively listen to and feel our own body sensations we can ultimately work in harmony with this inner guidance.

When in doubt, trust your instinct, the sensations, it can be your saviour when you are unable to pinpoint specific cues. Stay focussed on what is before you. Focus can unclutter the mind and you will be more than just a passive observer, you become an active observer with a clearer mind to tap into your inner guidance.

Active observation is a key ingredient to understanding body language. With focus, your conscious mind shifts to your subconscious and your subconscious mind will assist with interpreting skills without requiring active thought.

Silent Speech Flow

Body language just like written language has structure. Non-verbal expression flows, it has its own rhythm, vocabulary, grammar and punctuation. It all comes together with the cues of congruency, where words do not match non-verbal behaviours as well as the overall body of language.

Here is a scenario:

You are about to purchase a second-hand fridge you found listed in the for sale section of your local paper. You go to buy it and the person is dressed in neat and clean casual clothes, their tone of voice is compassionate with emphasis on being helpful to others, and this is why the fridge is really cheap. They present as a charitable humanitarian, they lean in too close, touch you on the forearm a few times and have unpleasant body odour. They appear friendly, yet there is an awkwardness about them and when they are not touching your forearm, their arms are crossed. Whilst you communicate verbally they interrupt, contradict you, and keep conversation going with little punctuation. This person has no reason to be dishonest, after all, the washing machine is so cheap, almost for free.

The rhythm of their body language expressed awkwardness, it also showed no breaks (punctuation) between touching your forearm and crossing of the arms. This did not match his verbal communication (vocabulary, grammar). His compassionate nature may be true however, his contradictions were words of superiority, not of a humble humanitarian, and with no punctuation indicating a sense of urgency.

His overall body language indicates that something must be wrong with the fridge, and though it still works it may not cool too well. The seller requires space and just wants a removalist to help dispose of the fridge.

Environment and Conditioned Belief

From birth we are taught by theories. A group of ideas and opinions about how something should be done, made, or thought about from our environment. Our environment includes relatives, community, school, audio, visual and all contact. Our interpretation of what we hear, see, smell, touch and taste as we grow is influenced by systematic arrangements from an immense network of experiences, and passed down from generations; and this becomes our conditioned belief system. Our identity and beliefs have formed from other people's opinions and now we are just like them. Our conditioned beliefs are also the culprits for our automatic body language.

We have an inherent understanding for the basics of body language, after all, primordial non-verbal language is deeply rooted in our subconscious and this is why we naturally use gestures while we talk. We also have the minds to master it. However, we learn body language much like the way we learn to speak and believe, by observation of our environment and then practice. Though we already have inherent understanding, good or successful body language is not something we are born with. It is through our associations in our environments that we consciously and unconsciously practiced imitating people around us; and applied the concept of monkey see, monkey do. If our associations and conditioned beliefs were and are of success then our body language will indicate successful outcomes, however, the opposite side of this can include struggle, just making ends meet, poverty or a mediocre life.

The good news is that conditioned success beliefs can be learned.

If there is a result we desire to experience in our life, and someone else has achieved it, we only need to observe and associate ourselves with this environment. It creates new neural pathways, new patterns... new automatic unconscious imprints. Our automatic body language right now and our experiences from past to present only exist because we repeated the practices of our environments. Through association, and repetition of association you can create new neural pathways that will overtake the old habits. Repetition is imperative to bring to us new, desired experiences. **Repetition Makes Permanent!**

Obstruction of time

When we aim in learning something new or recognise automatic habits and desire to change the unwanted involuntary expressions, we can often hear ourselves or others say, "It just takes time".

Einstein stated, *"Time is a concept that was created in the dim and distant past, yet, still we use it!"*

Regardless of us wanting this change, when we attach this utterly ridiculous concept of time to our desire, this places obstacle in our way, and can result in prolonging successful progress. If we hold a belief that things take time, our subconscious mind will ensure that this occurs by creating circumstances and events through our external expressions to extend the time, extend the time again, and extend the time even more, because the phrase 'it takes time' has no limit, the connotation attached to this belief is 'awhile'. Basically, whatever believe we will get the matching results.

Einstein's remark, *"yet, still we use it!"* shows us that time should be used for a purpose only. After all, time was created for purely one concept, and this concept was created a long while ago, well before we were born, and during the moment when the idea of time was created it served its purpose. A purpose that does not apply to us, we were not there!

Time is empty space, infinite, and has no meaning, nor has it any substance because it has no clear interpretation. There is no guidebook, it would be impossible to complete because how many volumes of books would there be for infinity. This ridiculous concept can have multitudes of definitions. For example. How long does it take someone to overcome sadness or how long does it take to learn something new? Is there a set way to reference length of time? NO! Because it varies for person to person, there is no definite meaning to time, it is an empty space of possibility, it cannot be estimated, and it all depends on how an individual perceives their possibilities. When someone believes they can learn quickly, they will. When someone believes they can go from sad to happy instantly, they CAN! It is utter rubbish to say "It takes time" because only the belief makes it so. DON'T BELIEVE things take time!

Posture Expression

Posture refers not only to how straight and erect our body is, it also includes orientation of the body, direction of the lean, and to what degree the body is open and inviting.

The natural spine has curves. The upper spine curves slightly backwards and lower back region curves slightly forward. Therefore, good posture does not mean that the body is straight and tall. What it does mean is that the spine is aligned and not twisted. This is called a neutral position where the weight of the body is held by the bones and not by the muscles, and our body can hold this posture without stressing joints, muscle and bones.

A neutral posture promotes ease of breathing, better circulation and balance. A spine that is not aligned can create discomfort, long term damage, or even deformities. While there are medical reasons for holding good posture, non-verbal reasons apply as well. Here are some examples:

Rounded shoulders indicate that a person is inactive in the conversation, this also applies to leaning away.

Poor posture associates to lack in confidence and to negative attributes such as; People that slump or habitually lean on their elbows while seated or against a wall express laziness or carelessness. Good or neutral posture indicates that one is in control, confident and powerful whereas, poor posture expresses being stiff, awkward, stressed, nervous and uncomfortable.

A component of posture is body orientation. This can also convey information when observing body language such as leaning. Leaning requires muscle work and balance, therefore when a person leans this is a significant non-verbal message, particularly when it is expressed by the torso. Here are some examples:

When weight is unevenly distributed across the legs this can indicate that a person is ready to leave a conversation such as slumping toward the exit door. This posture can alert you to knowing when it's time to end a conversation.

Leaning away from an entry/exit point conveys interest in the conversation. There are times where the body lean is subtler such as; while standing a person shifts their weight slightly forward; or the lean is directed to someone on their left or right. When someone is seated with the weight of their arms placed upon the knees, almost like a sprinter position they are absorbing as much information as possible.

When the brain chooses to evade others, the body will automatically react and we are often not aware of the expressions. This presents as inching away, and just a few inches indicates the onset of distancing, straying away from the conversation or getting ready to leave.

Upright neutral posture lengthens height whether standing or while seated. This is known as standing tall. To improve your posture, stand upright, push your shoulders up and back, ensure they are still relaxed. Align your neck with your spine, move your head back and level. Don't allow your head droop. Push your buttocks forward to shift weight onto your hips and legs. Tighten your stomach/solar plexus to assist your back and keep the torso straight and upright. Place arms to your sides with fingers loose and keep your body weight even across both feet.

Touch In Communication

A handshake, holding hands, kissing, high fiving, brushing up against someone, back slapping, or a pat all have significance. A touch can be used to soothe, to flirt, to express power and to maintain or indicate a bond.

Touching reveals intensity of emotions, cues such as; anger, fear, disgust, love, gratitude or sympathy, and these are dependent on the length, location on the body and type of touch.

Professionally, socially or in the workplace, the handshake is a universal form of touching and handshakes set the tone for the relationship. There are three main palm gestures during handshakes;

Palm down (dominance or superiority), emphasises that a person wishes to control and dominate by taking the superior position. This is similar to placing a hand on the shoulder, such as a father may do to let his child know who the boss is.

Palm up (submissiveness) and palm even (equality). Indicates allowing someone else to dominate.

Palm even or vertical indicates cooperation, equity in relationship and shows a desire to create a positive relationship. This is the most appropriate gesture for the handshake, especially on a first meeting.

Duration and pressure are two other important aspects of a good handshake. A handshake that is too short indicates lack of interest, warmth and enthusiasm, whereas a longer duration shows interest, attention and empathy. However, if the length of time increases too much, the positive can be replaced by the negative. When handshakes last too long the receiver may pull away slightly.

Testing pressure and duration is a great way to determine how strongly, someone will resist your authority. During the handshake add more pressure and increase the length of your handshake, if it's not met with additional pressure or is met with an attempt to pull away, you can be fairly certain that your demands will be met with little resistance.

More intimate forms of touching can include a friendly pat on the back to display encouragement or, a woman brushing up against a man with her body, indicates a desire for intimacy or courtship.

Pattern Interrupt and the Downtime Buffer

Pattern interrupt refers to movements that create relief, an energy adjustment. When someone is nervous or excited they find relief by; rubbing their legs with their hands (leg cleansing), rubbing their hands together or by stroking an object. Leg cleansing is a gesture that often goes unnoticed because it happens underneath a table, however, the upper body moves and this reveals the non-verbal language. Self-touching produces soothing neurochemicals.in our body to aid in relaxing stress and burns up the nervous energy.

Energy adjustment can be observed in many circumstances. People rub their hands together in excitement, wring their hands indicating agitation, under stress they pace, or even self-inflict pain such as ear pulling, hair pulling or scratching.

This adjustment creates a controlled release for tension and can be likened to a natural high that is achieved through physical exercise, except in this case it is a smaller dose of endorphin discharge, yet it still results in reduction of stress.

When a woman starts to stiffen, nervous about an issue, for example; where time is running out for a decision, they begin by crossing their arms then stroke their elbows or forearms. Their emotional change creates an uneasy feeling and if they stroke their body in a way that reminds them of a time when someone comforted them, this energy adjustment will relieve the emotions.

As for a male. Here is an example; a nervous husband waits outside a delivery room pacing back and forth. This energy adjustment gives him something to do and also burns up excess energy. Generally, a male's adjustment is easier to notice than a female because their body language will be rougher. Female body language will blend into their regular body language and can therefore be harder to spot.

In any moment, we can change our expressions regardless of our encompassing feelings; and relieve ourselves from restrictive beliefs including automatic body language. Einstein stated;

> *"The **only** reason for time is so that everything doesn't happen at once."*

Everything cannot happen at once. Though body language displays many cues, these cues have vacant seconds between them, known as the Downtime Buffer

Research shows that downtime, occurs roughly every three seconds whereby our minds 'slip away' and out of consciousness to give our minds the time it needs to relax and to be with our own thoughts. This 'downtime' also internalises and processes the information that is happening around us; and gives us the required pause to think about what we want to say or do next. For this reason, it is important that we pause occasionally and avoid using speech continuously. The voice distracts from this process. Even though the buffer is still occurring we cannot be mindful of this pause while the verbal sound is drowning it.

Back to Pattern interrupt to create relief, with the energy adjustment:

Choose one pattern, one frequency for energy adjustment. Pattern interrupts can include; humming, physical movements such as walk, jump, skip, clap your hands, dance, shake your body, touch an object, or self-touching. All these stimulate the neurochemicals. Inhaling through the nose and exhaling from the mouth will reset the frequency (feeling) or bypass the automatic, unconscious imprints. Your breath is your physical life force, place focus on it when you are nervous, anxious or tense. Always take in to consideration the circumstances you are in and select a pattern interrupt that does not present as inappropriate body language for that circumstance.

When you feel relief, express some body language that is conducive for how you wish the circumstance to play out. Your wish as and when you command.

Conditioned beliefs are the governors for automatic reaction, and the why, why in some circumstances we see ourselves inferior or unworthy; including positive aspects such as smart, friendly or happy. Recognize your memory as something that contains missing pieces and remember, it plays no relevance in what you require in new situations. After all, there are many other possibilities, you may not have experienced or learned from your environment. Therefore, you can draw from whatever pleases you.

Many gestures can be used for energy adjustment and this varies for the individual. Any movement that has no immediate function and is expressed when faced with stress can be called energy adjustment. By observing others and yourself during these adjustments you can compile a list of these cues for future reference. When you do observe these signals in action, an appropriate response is to offer comfort, however, if it is displayed in a professional situation, or during a sale, then it is usually time to retreat and allow them time to think things over. It is best practice to allow someone who under stress, some time to reach a conclusion on their own, without interference.

Chapter 5
Opened Mind, Closed Mind

Knowing the difference between open postures and closed postures is important when determining the thoughts, feelings and moods of others. Open body language corresponds to openness of the mind and people are more welcoming to outside views. Closed postures are of course, a closed mind, and these people have no interest in new ideas.

Posture for openness presents as; body is relaxed, unbuttoned collars, ties removed, pants may hang loose. The centre-line of the body is free from obstruction from any limbs or objects.

Closed posture present as; tense muscles, a limb comes across the centre of the body and locks with the opposite leg, or when the arms fully cross over one another. The centre-line of the body is obstructed by limbs or objects. When closed postures are combined with other closed postures, the signal is very noticeable. Here's an example: Legs and arms are crossed in combination with an expressionless face, turning away, and a sense that communication is not welcomed at any level.

When someone has their legs crossed yet their arms are open and honest this can indicate a deliberate and conscious attempt to appear relaxed, when in fact they are not, or, that someone has mixed feelings and is reserved at one level, but open at another level. These are conflicting cues and these cues tell us that someone has an internal reservation or collision, hence their mixed message.

Abdominal Defence

Exposing our abdomen and pelvic region indicates trust. Trust in knowing that we are safe and beyond attack. We choose safe zones such as our homes or healing centres when laying on our backs and this is because it exposes our body to attack; and in this pose our body is compromised, somewhat paralysed to defend ourselves, therefore we use shields.

Arm and leg crossing is indicative of shielding, this can be from physical and emotional threats. A body may turn away from another indicating lack of trust, or distancing the torso, this shows someone preparing space in case a threat amplifies, and then the shield for escape is ready. When someone does not like what they are hearing, they slouch or lean backward indicating they do not see eye-to-eye on the topic of discussion. The bored or disinterested will also slouch or sit awkwardly low and to one side on their seats ready to take flight.

Abdomen and pelvic distancing can also be a cue for agreement. When in agreeance, both communicators move toward each other to lessen the distance. When an audience shows interest and are keen, they sit on the edge of their seat, exposing their abdomen and absorb every word.

When in conversation, people orientate their abdomen and pelvic region toward those they trust, favour and with whom they agree with most. When oriented away, this indicates those they trust least, people they disagree with or have contempt for. Slight disagreements, topics of no interest or topics we do not want to discuss can orientate the abdomen and pelvic region away from the speaker as well.

When we trust and love others, such as family, we openly expose our abdomen and pelvic area. For example; when we hug, we move our arms away from the front of the body to get closer for pressing the torsos together. Children permit people they trust such as parents or family members to blow sounds onto their stomachs, known as raspberries. However, even children will turn their backs to us when they are upset or when we enforce rules. This is a non-verbal indication showing disagreement.

Orientation can change over the course of a conversation as ideas and emotions digress such as; when dating, if someone is displeased they will first shift their feet toward the exit, followed by the torso. They will attempt to appear polite, and maintain facial contact, yet the rest of their body is indicating that they are preparing to leave.

Intimate partners in deep conversations will move in closer and face one another indicating trust, as well as no desire to exit, if the torso is turned away a desire to exit is indicated. When a torso is oriented forward this is the direction someone is thinking of moving towards, and when lovers do this, it indicates they wish to move into one another; and to kiss.

During a professional circumstance, when someone/s agrees with you they turn their body so that they may closely face you, even while sitting. In contrast, for those whom they disagree with, they pull back slightly and turn their body away.

Use non-verbal language that reflects the feelings you want to convey in circumstances. The best abdomen/pelvic body language is to lean forward and drop the arms to the side to project agreement. If you disagree, simply lean back or lean back and towards the side on a chair; or turn to a side and cross the arms.

Hands and Palms

Non-verbal communication during primordial era taught us to be fixated on what our hands were doing. They were used for gestures in language, for creating, catching and collecting. Due to this inherent fixation the brain has shown to place a priority and a high portion of attention towards the wrists, palms, and fingers, more so than other parts of the body.

Being honest relates to being open and without hiding anything. The palm relays important gestures that signifying honesty, palms that face down, tell, and palms up, offer. Here are examples;

Palm up - Exposing Palm and wrists in an upward direction indicates sexual or erotic displays and is often expressed by women during courtship. A wave of the hand indicates a long distance greeting, Open palms facing up, indicates openness and equality. Open gestures often include phrases such as; trust me, would I lie to you, or, you don't believe me. Arms out and extended, palms up, or vertical indicates that we are safe. The stretch to which this openness occurs indicates how open someone is such as; arms to the side/up and open with fingers apart signals complete openness. Palms facing upward indicates we are offering something. However, the offering is a notion, rather than something tangible. Arms completely outstretched with palms up, or prayer-like, is not dominant nor confidant and indicates offering a dialogue to another and sincerely wanting to be believed, trusted and accepted. Palm flashes show honesty and trustworthiness also indicating no threat, they lack power in terms of conviction though.

Palm down- Hands facing down on a table or standing and leaning with the fingertips spread to anchor the body indicates empathy and confidence. When you want to allow, admit or surrender, face the palms down. To display honesty, such as a declaration, 'believe me, I didn't do it' use the palm down gesture this indicates telling of truth.

Hands deep in a pocket or behind the back signal aggression, passive threat, and that someone is hiding something. When children lie they conceal their hands by placing them behind their back. However, hands in the pocket can also indicate feeling more comfortable and a way to occupy our hands or wanting to tell (admit). With this gesture it is better to group together other signals from the body language. Hidden hands convey lack in confidence especially when there is a flow in other suitable gestures during a conversation.

Hands are an effective way for us to present as more honest and intelligent people. At a subconscious level, when our palms are made more visible by showing more flesh, the more honest others will find us, the speaker.

Here are some more gestures:
Hands are parallel to one another moving up and down as if measuring an object signals a desire to project thoughts onto others.
Hands held out, fingers fanned apart and the palm facing an audience is an expression to make contact with the audience.
Hands and palm up as if giving a gift is a beggar's plea where someone is desperately wanting agreement from the audience.
Arms form a circle in front of the body with palms facing inward toward the speaker indicates that the speaker wants the audience to accept their way of thinking.
Hands with palm up in a stop motion indicates the speaker wants the audience to settle or calm so the speech can continue.

Changes in the hands

Whenever there is sudden change in hand gestures, an emotion or thought has changed, and it is usually tied directly to whatever is happening in the moment.

When a conversation detours to a disagreement between people, hands pull inward and away from the other in this disagreement. This can occur suddenly, particularly during a heated topic. When disagreement is present, the body will also be withdrawn and the hands resting on the lap. If an argument continues, both parties move hands away, the feet orient toward the door, the torso follows and the head.

If someone changes thought during a topic, their hands can remain outstretched, but the palms turn upwards to offer the idea, or to change the mind of the listener.

Arms withdraw for many reasons: The subconscious mind triggers flight response and pulls hands in when someone feels hurt even when fear of being hurt is felt. Touching a hot surface, the sound of a loud bang, when we are worried, or a verbal threat will cause our arms to draw back quickly to protect our hands. This is an automatic response that cannot be stopped because our mind feels an attack must been blocked.

Hands just as arms withdraw for many reasons: Honest hands present as palm up, offering something to another, even palm down in a confident authoritative position, however, when hands are pulled away, this indicates hidden thoughts of disagreement and lack of connectivity.

When hands pause, stop or the use of them slows this indicates being caught in a lie. A liar will use this freeze response to seem less noticeable because less movement attracts less attention. When hands that are usually busy when talking begin to slow, or become less expressive, can indicate lack of enthusiasm or confidence for the topic of conversation.

Hand Rubbing

Rubbing the hands together indicates that someone is preparing to receive something such as; a sale, winning a prize or expectation of something. There are variations of emotions for hand rubbing, for example, rubbing the hands slowly with a smug smile expresses a devious intention. This may be a salesperson slowly rubbing their hands as they formulate a plan for higher sales at your expense. Slow hand rubbing often indicates that good is coming to the person expressing this gesture, whereas rubbing quickly indicates benefits for more than one person, for example, a salesperson may have two suitable items for sale, however, one is higher in profit, while the other is more suitable for the buyer. If hand rubbing slows for one item over the other, this indicates which they would rather sell. Always be watchful when someone rubs their hands slowly, it implies that other benefits at our expense, and the slower, more concealed the rubbing becomes, the more cautious we should be.

Finger Pointer and Power Gestures

The pointer can be depicted as a spear thrower. When someone thrusts their finger forward they are jabbing their ideas onto you. The finger is also used in an up and down motion indicating beating down upon an opponent and creating obedience. The pointed finger indicates a very negative emotion and presents during an aggressive verbal argument for personal attacks against another. Pointing reflects responsibility onto the listener, creates defensive emotions and as it persists the listener becomes aggressive. As for the one who is pointing this creates negative ramifications. Finger pointing is a lose/lose gesture, and therefore best to avoid.

An abbreviated gesture for pointing is the thumb in hand gesture. The thumb and index finger touch and the other fingers form a ball. The hand then motions as if pointing, emphasising speech with conviction. This gesture is less offensive than the pointing finger. Another gesture considered to be thought provoking and honest that places responsibility on the speech is the Okay gesture. This presents as the thumb against the index finger forming a circle with the remaining fingers pointed upwards. The Okay signal rotated so the fingers face the listener and the thumb parallel to the chest, indicates precision and delicacy. However, when the thumb and index finger come close, but do not touch, is a gesture to express when posing questions rather than making statements.

Another gesture is the hammer fist where the hand tenses into a ball to repeatedly hammer an idea to listeners. The hammer fist shows conviction and determination. When the fingers are curled lightly not quite forming a fist, this indicates mild power and a desire to be taken seriously but this lacks the conviction expressed by the hammer fist.

Arms and Legs

Frowning requires more muscles and effort than smiling and our natural, default facial expression is the smile. Alike the smile, openness in body language is our default expression because a tense or closed body requires more effort and motivation. Motivation can come from fearful or unwanted stimulus that triggers the fight or flight reaction and this is a predictor for unpleasant outcomes.

Being open profiles comfortable positions, such as; stretching our arms out, hands above the head, spreading our legs open or even laying down completely, unlike the muscle tightness and constriction we feel when we close posture. With open gestures, the cerebral cortex, the part of our brain that aids in judgment, is disrupted from producing depressive stimulators, instead it increases verbal communication and makes us feel more confident.

Closed body language expresses when a limb crosses the midpoint of the body. Also, during leg and arm crossing, and this affects blood circulation, as well as a physical healing such as wounds, tissue repair or regeneration of internal organs. With open body language we may be exposed to circumstances, yet we have no fear of harm. Our body is relaxed without requiring action or effort, and it is in a natural, default expression. Open body language is also loose, arms sway freely, we have no concerns about humility or of being attacked, and arms or legs are un-crossed leaving the torso and groin area exposed.

Crossing Arms

Arms in body language represent shields. When we fold the arms across the body we close our body language, and unconsciously disturb breath flow and blood circulation to our vital organs, the heart and lungs. This shielding indicates protection from physical attack as well as protection from undesirable views others are expressing. Therefore, arms across the chest can indicate that a physical or emotional threat is being felt. Arms crossed in a meeting or conversation indicates defensiveness, negativity, uncertainty and insecurity, as well as disagreement whilst a question is being asked. When in public areas, arm crossing presents due to the stress of being in a non-comfort zone environment, indicating insecurity. When someone is resistant to flirtation or intimate pursuit from another, they will express an arm cross to preserve their personal space and to repel sexual advances.

Research has shown that we use arm crossing positions because there is an underlying emotion attached to it and it is the emotion that actually creates discomfort in the gesture. Unlike some other gestures, that may have alternate reasons, arm crossing only indicates closed body language. To avoid closed body postures, we must first eliminate the root source of the emotion and then open posture will come naturally.

Arm crossing also presents in other ways to shield, not only the arm cross. These gestures can also indicate; protection, defence, negativity, uncertainty, resistance and insecurity. Here are some examples:

One arm resting, stretched out, in front of the torso, upon a table; with the opposite hand on the wrist or forearm.
The arm upright and holding a drink in the hand.
Crossing one leg over the knee and the ankle locks it to the other leg.
A Full self-embrace with the arms unlocked.
The hand crosses subtly and grabs the opposite wrist.
Hand pretends to alleviate an itch.

Though most closed body cues indicate that a negative attitude is present, there can be varying signals. For example, full arm crossing with a poker face (blank expression), a tense, firm or hostile posture, and limbs that appear indicates total rejection (very negative attitude). However, unsettled closed signals where some blocking is present, a semi-relaxed position, a neutral face and slight movement of arms and hands, can imply that an offer or agreement is being considered. Rather than a no, they are indicating a maybe or I'll think about it.

A hand reaching over the opposite side of the body to grab the elbow or shoulder also indicates, a maybe or a chance is possible. However, if there is a hostile facial expression, arms tightly folded across the chest, and the head tilted sideways, then there is no interest in listening.

Studies have shown that a significant amount of information is stopped from reaching the brain when closed body language is expressed. Therefore, when verbally communicating to anyone who has arms crossed it would be useful to aid them to open up and change the negative cues. This will increase comprehension and recall of your message, it also has a higher chance for agreement. This is why is it important to adjust our approach when someone has their arms crossed. To reshape or change this expression we can present a pattern interrupt. For example; have them stand up and move next to you or pass something over to them where they are prompted to reach forward. This creates a ready position with their bodies leaning toward you. If their arms are crossed, ask them to write notes about the information you provide, or hand them a document and ask them view it. Ensure you observe the body language after any pattern interrupt to assess if they have returned to their original closed body position. If this occurs then they have no interest in your message.

Other ways to open profiles include; handing over a cup of coffee or glass of water, showing photographs, or simply passing over something they expressed interest in. Handing over any object instantly cues someone to uncross their arms, reach for it and therefore opening body language. Whatever object is selected for the pattern interrupt is not important, it just requires to be interesting enough to motivate them in reaching over.

Crossing the Legs

Legs are equally as expressive as arms. While the arms are occupied with gestures, this distracts from the legs, therefore legs whether sitting or standing are free to express hidden thoughts.

Legs are an indicator of true thoughts and feelings. For example, men may look at women's legs to verify interest. Crossing legs toward something or someone indicates an attraction in that direction.

Legs automatically aim in the direction in which we think. Loving couples cross their legs toward each other, and enemies cross away. A couple on a couch with legs crossed toward each other, bodies leaning inward, with arms touching on the back of the couch is known as a loving circle; and this expression is not just for intimate couples, it also applies to family, friends, and even associates, both male and female. It indicates likeness of mind or agreement.

Studies show that when someone is being untruthful, movement of the feet increases significantly, and this movement is expressed automatically and unconsciously. A leg tap, where the hand taps the thigh indicates uneasiness, boredom, fear or deceit, even the fear of being caught. This gesture is dependent on other cues and on the context.

Uncrossed legs signal openness, acceptance and of being easy going. However, this can be viewed as a sexual signal, an invitation, or it can indicate power play. When someone wants to display a signal of dominance and authority, or to appear open, their legs are uncrossed along with gestures such as; throwing an arm over the back of the chair to take up more space and use loud boisterous verbal behaviour. When a leg is tossed over the arm rest this indicates quarrelsome intentions or a chip on the shoulder.

The greater the leg spread, the greater the dominance display. The legs raised and at shoulder width while seated, indicates comfort and a natural state, however if the legs widen to their maximum distance, this is a cue for yelling and begging to be noticed. When one ankle is placed on top of the opposite knee this indicates unassuming and less dominance. Legs crossed over the knee tightly shows a respectful, polite and proper attitude.

In a standing position, legs spread slightly beyond shoulder width signals dominance, however, this is viewed as more acceptable because it expresses openness, acceptance and confidence. Crossing at the ankles, indicates a cautious mind and therefore is a closed posture. We must be attentive when observing leg information because people have a preferred way to cross them. By watching the movement along with context, we can reach are more genuine conclusion.

Ankle Cross

While seated or standing this posture presents as ankles crossing each other. It can also present as a leg raised to the back calve like a flamingo. The ankle cross indicates; holding a negative emotion, uncertainty, fear, feelings of discomfort or threat, stress, anxiety, insecurity or timidity. It also shows reservation and self-restraint. Ankles cross due to a subconscious freeze response or threat, the legs entwine to restrict and restraint movement.

While seated, when legs are locked behind the legs of a chair, signals a restraining, freeze like expression. This posture indicates lack in confidence and is an unnatural position. This coupled with interlocked legs, with pacifying behaviours such as rubbing the thighs with palm down, as if to dry them, is a bundling signal indicating that a secret is being covered. If the feet move beneath a chair, this projects exaggeration because the feet reveal truth, this shows closed body language and one has withdrawn from the conversation, rather than hiding a secret. Be observant of this posture when verbalising a controversial opinion as it indicates disagreement, and more so if this posture is held for a length in time.

Just as closed arm and leg postures, ankle cross is a closed posture. Create a pattern interrupt when possible, some examples can be; have them change positions, stand or relocate to a more comfortable seating location, or you identify and address the issue of concern. Simply asking the reason for the reservation can aid in eliminating this posture because a person feels they are being heard. Allowing the opportunity to express thoughts and feelings triggers people in feeling that someone is willing to listen and oftentimes this is all that is required to open someone up. After all, this is a posture of hidden disagreement, and it would be hard to hold the posture when one is given the chance to open up. If this posture returns during communication, this indicates that true opinion has not been fully disclosed, or that a new issue has presented.

Hand Lock and Four leg Cross

A four leg cross presents as; one leg bent and pulled over the opposite knee, to form the number four. This is an open posture and indicates; a person is relaxed, youthful in attitude and dominant. However, this can be a closed posture when each hand rests palms down on the legs (known as hand lock) and indicates; stubbornness, a highly opinionated nature that rejects opinions of others and the possibility of a disagreement. This hand lock is stronger as a signal when a negative facial expression is present such as a scowl, or frown. If you observe this body language it is best to retreat. A stubborn person is not often willing to drop their guard once they have begun.

The Fig Leaf

This is closed body position and blocks the mid-section from view by placing one or both hands in front of the lower abdomen, genitals or chest. Much like where a fig leaf would be placed. A modest person undressing will instinctively clasp their hands over their private areas if someone enters. Women divide this signal with one arm and hand for breasts, and the other hand over genitals.

Even though we are not naked and exposed in public, our minds will respond to exposure with feelings of insecurity. This gesture presents as both hands clasping with interlocking fingers, or hand upon hand; and placed over a mid-section of the body. Standing is a common position for this gesture, yet it can present when seated where hands are rested on the lap. When a woman crosses their arms in front of their chest this can indicate feeling threatened, therefore they create a barrier or block from view with objects such as a book, a jacket, a handbag or scarf.

This posture shows insecurity and can present when someone is in an environment or around people they are not familiar with, and can present when speakers lack confidence, particularly in front of a large audiences or when someone requires assistance to relay a concept.

Parallel Legs

This is a sign of femininity as it is a posture that can be uncomfortable for male genitals and male hips are usually narrower than the hips of a female. The parallel legs posture presents as; one leg pressed against the other making the legs appear toned, sexier and more youthful. This sitting position is often expressed when a woman is wanting to draw sexual attention to themselves.

Pigeon Toes

Toes pointed inwards are often called pigeon toes. This is submissive body language that makes the body appear smaller and expresses a non-threatening posture. Someone was is infatuated with another will point their toes inwards indicating timidness and willingness to be dominated. In a sexual situation, it reflects servitude indicating another is in charge.

Submission is present everywhere such as; the workplace between employee and employer, our homes, someone wears the pants or is the head of the table. Power imbalances exist in the world around us, and often this is necessary, someone needs to take charge while others follow. This is how we achieve consumer results and advancements in areas such as technology, science or the wellness industry.

Hidden Standing Positions

There are four common ways in which a person stands; straight with feet together, feet parallel and slightly apart, one foot forward and the fourth, legs crossed at the ankle.

Legs straight with feet together- This is an attentive posture used as obedience. It is a neutral, honest pose and is expressed in circumstances with differing status such as; a boss and employee, or parent and child.

Feet parallel and slightly apart- Legs are spread at shoulder width while standing and indicates 'going nowhere'. This expression can be empowered by placing thumbs in a belt (cowboy pose)

One foot forward- This indicates subtle interest toward the direction in which the foot is pointed. To show interest, the foot forwards the speaker. Foot away from the speaker and toward another direction indicates who one would rather speak to, or to if at a door, ending the conversation is desired. The foot takes the first step toward where the mind wishes it to be.

Legs crossed at the ankle- This is a submissive posture revealing that someone is not ready to commit to a concept, is not ready to leave, yet doubt is felt in the situation. The ankle cross is a subconscious denial to access the mind. Our mind and body are linked therefore when we uncross our limbs we express that we are willing to listen and participate. When another uncrosses with you, it is an indication that your opinions match, or there is a willingness to consider your words.

An open posture when standing expresses supreme confidence as it exposes the midsection to attack. Often when people first meet, they show timidity by crossing at the ankle. Those exempt from this usually carry a higher status and are aware of their body language.

Releasing Our Guard

A defensive and timid posture is a natural, inherent habit expressed when people meet, this presents as closed or protective body language. Arms or legs crossed at the ankles is a common gesture for most, children in particular can express closed body language with first meetings as they feel they are lower in status, and those who view themselves higher in status will naturally express fewer closed postures.

Our automatic impulse for guarding ourselves presents as; the body tenses and shows certain levels of awkwardness. When strangers meet, they signal with arms folded across the chest, or hands in pockets with legs crossed at the ankle. This is also dependent on someone's level of comfort of the circumstance, environment and the how they perceive status of others in attendance.

As a meeting continues, feet are the first to separate and uncross at the ankle. They move to a, 'at attention' stance (a few inches apart from the other). And this can occur in unison with all in attendance. The arms express next, they become animated to relay the verbal language. The palms are more visible showing honesty and openness. The arms remain uncrossed and become more active in conversation yet, they can still be placed in pockets indicating lingering reservation or be placed on hips to signal dominance if someone identifies as having a higher status. Finally, if resonance and agreement is reached, one foot extends toward the other person rather than at an exit. The physical distance reduces with a step forward, or brief touching may occur on the forearm or elbow.

If first impressions are ineffective and seen as negative the conversation can become more awkward and body language will increase in tension, then methods will be used to exit the conversation. If one person fails to express open posture, usually both won't. This process is known as mirroring each other and is an automatic, natural development with communication. Occasionally, one person will open up, and the other not, signalling a one-way agreement, or one person is more open minded and easy to please than the other.

Eyes

Eyes can signal that someone has closed body language. Here are some examples; The head turns to avoid being singled out, or the chin pulls in and head tucks down to protect the vulnerable neck from attack indicating a fearful state.

A lack of direct eye contact during conversation is not always a negative cue or rejection. Research has shown that concentrating upon a face requires effort. Therefore, when we look away it is in order to analyse and process what is being said. Looking away is also a signal that we are comfortable and trust the people with us, this is because we feel we can safely look away without risk of being attacked.

The contrast between eye avoidance and a comfort signal is quite obvious. For example, eyes looking down, focusing on picking dirt from beneath the nails, removing lint from clothing while avoiding a topic, or gazing without expression in boredom is not the same as looking away during a conversation to focus and process more deeply. This type of eye avoidance is often acceptable, however, during a job interview, it is preferred that candidates focus on the interviewer rather than gazing about the room, as freely moving eyes leave bad impressions and make potential employees appear disinterested.

Fetal Position

This is an extreme expression of closed posture, as well as insecurity and can present as; hugging knees curling up in a ball, or limbs pulled in closer to the body and across the centre-line (a self-hug). As we age, the fetal position, like thumb sucking, is viewed as an unacceptable way for dealing with insecurity therefore, extreme gestures evolve to more subtle cues such as; playing with hair by rolling it around a finger or sucking on it, sucking on a pen, or sucking the fingers with emphasis and sound after a meal. .

Openness and Status

Openness is an expression of comfort and being closed relates to fear of attack. Dominant people express open postures and people who view themselves as inferior express closed postures.

Someone that is comfortable in the workplace expresses as; hands to the sides and arms not crossed, a palm down handshake is used indicating dominance and higher status.

An employee that views themselves as lower in status; leans against objects such as a desk to hold themselves up, hide behind objects like coffee mugs or folders, place hands in pockets, and find refuge against the back of a chair. They may also express a partial arm cross, by grabbing the opposite arm or elbow, and tucking one leg behind the other.

Chapter 6
Foundation of Body Language Comfort/Discomfort

Body language helps us to understand one another. If you encounter a friend and their body language shows sadness, you now know that you can assist in easing their discomfort with a pattern interrupt. When you are speaking and someone's body language shows interest, you now know to keep talking. These are examples of the two fundamental signals which are the bases for body language; "comfort" and "discomfort."

Comfort signals tell us that a person is feeling good. People signal comfort when they like the person they are interacting with, they enjoy the current activity or interaction, and there is nothing troubling them.

Discomfort signals tell us that something is wrong. Such as; something personal is bothering them, when they are unhappy, or they are not enjoying their current activity, interaction or company.

Open and closed body language can signal a desire to allow or deny access to the body. Abdominal and pelvic displays show us that someone is open and trusting however, this response is difficult when emotions are hidden. Comfort is expressed through distance and people do this by moving their body closer or leaning towards rather than away from another, they will also remove objects that impede their view so as to establish more intimacy.

Comfortable people have fluid, loose bodies rather than inflexibility. They gesture with speech instead of freezing or appearing awkward. Sometimes they will slow verbal communication to produce accurate answers. Comfortable people mirror others instead of avoiding synchronicity, breath rate and postures will be similar, instead of showing differences.

Positive body language is expressed by people who are more in control and attentive instead of appearing vulnerable, they talk, express in multiple ways and genuinely smile. Fake smiles are an expression that can be used to disguise stress, however, a phony smile lasts much longer than a natural, honest smile, because when someone is positive, speech slots in between the smile. Therefore, it is easy to recognise.

A body shows discomfort by increased heart rate, breath rate or sweating. A change in normal face or neck colour can present, as well as, trembling or shaking hands, compressing the lips, fidgeting, drumming fingers and other repetitive behaviours. Voices often crack when under stress, mouths dry showing noticeable swallowing or frequent throat clearing. Cues to detect lying can include objects as barriers. For example, hiding parts of their face with drinking glasses or when standing using walls and chairs to lean against to gain support. Liars engage in eye avoidance by covering their eyes or squint to stop what is being said from entering their minds. When eyes begin to flutter or express constant blinking this indicates an internal struggle.

Lack of touching also signals discomfort and a separation from ideas. When ideas differ, it can be difficult to participate with others, and this can bring about a fear response. Head movements that are inconsistent with speech such as slight nodding, yet words depict denial (and vice versa), or delaying head nodding until after speech indicates lack in synchronicity and can expose liars. When gestures present out of sync it reveals that a person is adding the gesture only as a convincing support for their statement. When nodding presents during denial statements such as nodding "yes" whilst saying "I did not do it" this often very subtle. In observing these cues look at possible reasons for the discomfort or stress rather than the lie. Discomfort or stress can create a lie, therefore, attempt to establish why a person is feeling this way. Is it because they are being put on the spot, they fear being misjudged, or because they are actually telling lies?

Stress automatically expresses in body language such as picking lint to signal detachment from a conversation, it also displays in shifting gestures such as scratching the body, rubbing the neck or wiping the side of the nose. A palm up can indicate that a person has some doubt, it can also indicate a desire for another to believe them, and in contrast the palm down reveals confidence and authority.

Micro expressions can also be revealing, such as an eye, eyebrow or corner mouth twitch. They occur instantaneously, subconsciously and disappear quickly. To observe micro expressions, pay attention to initial movements, particularly when they are negative, as these are more honest than positive body language.

Comfort and Discomfort Response

These signals are the clues that tell us how another is feeling. Once we know how someone is feeling, we know how to respond. Think of these signals as red light/green light. 'I'm feeling comfortable' indicates a green light and when this is expressed, you can relax and enjoy the interaction. Be mindful though, in case body language changes to discomfort, otherwise, continue relaxing and doing whatever you were doing. A red light signals, 'I'm not comfortable' (or, a yellow "Caution" light.). This is a signal for us to help our listener feel more comfortable. Attempt to establish the cause for the discomfort, and see if you can transmute is to comfort.

Comfort and Discomfort Signals

Expression of discomfort can signal when a long-winded answer is given rather than a desired short response. This is common due to the fact that people feel polite, intelligent or friendly communication means to use verbal language, therefore they babble on while we sit through a massive speech of useless, routine information and irrelevant opinions. When verbally communicating, cut long-winded explanations short, use less words often, LESS IS MORE, and only use words that are relevant to the circumstance or people before you. This way you will be rewarded with comfortable body language.

Comfort and discomfort is communicated to us through body language all the time and at every moment. Learn to understand these body language signals as well as context, pause and take advantage of the three second downtime buffer so you may process any circumstances, then you can think about what say or do next and respond appropriately; and… magically transform any interaction into successful and positive outcomes for all included. However, what does respond appropriately really mean? Well it all hangs on foundations and in understanding why LESS IS MORE is immensely important.

Illuminating and Activating Words

Before we go into "less is more" it is important to know what we are doing when speaking and why words are imperative to our desired life results. The following has excerpts from another book I wrote, *Festival Of The imagination.*

Thoughts, emotions and **WORDS** are energy; they consist of matter (particles) that can be measured, even seen in science. When words are spoken they carry with them conscious intent to bring into our physical experience the exact match of the frequency we relay.

When a word is first created it first appears as a concept in thought. The inventor of any particular word imagined this concept and in that same moment they also had a particular sensation (emotion), just as we all have emotions in every moment. We are never without emotional sensation. When the inventor expanded on the concept with thought, they added alphabetic combination to create a sound. This sound and the emotion felt by the inventor in that moment merge and create a pattern, a pattern of a unique frequency and this now invented word originates into another 'something' that has conscious intent. Whatever words we use in conversation carry the frequency of the merged conscious intent of the time of invention. We must be thoughtful and selective of the words we use, as these unique frequencies will be matched by our subconscious and bring into our life experience these exact results through emotions, habits, attitudes and non-verbal expression.

An old Chinese proverb and stated this well:

> *"Watch your thoughts for they become words.*
> *Watch your words for they become actions.*
> *Watch your actions for they become habits.*
> *Watch your habits for they become your character.*
> *And watch your character for it becomes your destiny.*
> *What we think, and say we become."*

The conscious intent or unique frequency (purpose, goal and end result) of any word can be distorted, veiled or muffled when used in the wrong context with the unique frequency of another word/s. Therefore, it is essential for us to be mindful of context, correct word and sound as an important part of our language when we are to choose exactly what we want.

All words have origins. Many English words have been borrowed from others known as root or origin words, for example; Anglo-Saxon, German, Greek, Latin, or French. And the root words are the ones that hold power (unique frequency), immense power, when they were created.

The words we speak or write come from our thoughts. Whether the words are spoken, thought or written they impact our outcomes in life, and regardless of what new or expanded definition is attached to them, the only frequency that counts is the sound and the original meaning of the word. When we don't use a word in context to the original meaning we confine our possibilities, and this can block our path to abundance.

When a word is used in its correct context with its original meaning this is known as illuminating and activating. This is a critical key when speaking, thinking or writing words, particularly for desired outcomes.

Many words have had contrasting and altered definitions applied throughout the years. We use many words and often we are unaware to the true and initial definition which carry the merged emotions and conscious intent. We only know the definition that was passed onto us, and what we read in the remodeled dictionaries. Here are a few examples of original words and the altered definitions;

Fun: from verb *fun* (1680s) "to cheat, hoax." Altered: "Something that provides mirth or amusement: enjoyment or playfulness."

Awesome: from *awe* (n.) + *-some*. "Fear causing or terror causing." Altered: Slang "very impressive."

'Awe': from c.1300, *aue*, "fear, terror, great reverence,"

'–Some': from Old English *–sum*, "tending to; causing; to a considerable degree."

Lady: from Old English *hlæfdige* "one who kneads bread." Altered: "A woman who is refined, polite, and well-spoken." Hmm. I think I'll pass on being called a lady. I don't particularly see myself as a bread kneader.

Every sound we convey and every word we think sends out a frequency, an energy stream that creates our reality. We attract like energy, like attracts like, the Law of Attraction. And because of tampered definitions and lack in awareness, we are either improving or destroying our health, relationships, or our prosperity automatically. Our subconscious is listening to our transmissions, disregarding whether we know or do not know what the frequency means, and giving us what we ask for, every time.

Success in all areas of life comes in part from communication with our thoughts, to ourselves, to and from others. We use words to relay these thoughts, concepts, ideas, images and intentions. It is essential that we develop an awareness of our words as well as the way we and others around us use language by practising words as they were designed to be used and understand what particular outcomes they carry. We can choose to Define with the truest definition or stay on automatic and Confine our ability to create joy, success and abundance.

Words are a command to our thoughts and this IS a way we create energy (frequency). When we speak, we also think, which doubles the transmission with the Law of Attraction. To forward our opportunity towards success we can choose to quit (release, let go) using the words that hold us back and replace them with power words that will serve us well. Words that will increase and align our energetic experience. Because, everything is energy. Including words!

Our practised interpretations passed onto us from our environment are either helping, hampering or even blocking our easy path to success and we do this unconsciously. Take back the control of the energies you emit with your words. Start by writing a list of the common phrases and words you use then research the origin. Understand these words you use including those voiced by others. Gain comprehension of the true meaning as well as pronunciation in order to unleash the power of words you choose, and this will cooperate in creating what you desire rather than a blockage of your success. When you come across a powerful word, use it repeatedly. I often say 'wonderful' and find no need to speak any other word to describe: *full of or having marvelous things and miracles.* And when I speak or journal, I use the word as wunderfoll. As it was originally intended.

When you next speak, listen to what you are actually transmitting. As the old adage goes, "be careful what you wish for."

I was surprised when I began to explore the origins and meanings of words that I used often. I explored this further with a friend who is a wordsmith, one who is an expert with words. We both were astounded to find a significant amount of words we assumed to know the definitions to, and discovered we were clouded by the influences of environments, this includes; the beliefs and interpretations shared to us from our families, schools, friends, colleagues, advertising, basically the environment surrounding us from past to present. And it is this absence of awareness that can create our unwanted experiences. Here are some powerful words to get you started for better experiences:

Power words: Accept (*accepter*), faith (*faith, feith, fei, fai*), love (*lufu*), hilarious (*hilaris*), joy (*joie*), supreme (*superus*), bliss (*blis*), bless (*bletsian*), tranquillity (*tranquilite*), absolute (*absolut*), achieve (*achever*), worthy (*axios*), *magic (magique*), happy/wealth (*ead*), abundance *(abundare),* feel *(felan),* good *(god- say with long 'o),* perfect *(parfiten,* creative *(creatus).*

Power phrases: For my gain. Super serene, Bright eyes, Guidance from the angels.

"Words are free. it's how you use them that may cost you." – Kushand

"Handle them carefully, for words have more power than atom bombs."- Ira Gassen

You do not need a large vocabulary to create your desired life. There are successful people who are illiterate, and those who have wealth, health and happiness with very small vocabularies. Heed the advice from some wise masters throughout the centuries, "use less words" or "less is more."

Less IS More

Balanced speaking and listening is as imperative just as rehydrating our body with water or breathing in order to attain successful results in any communication.

People try to cram too much data into their talks. They often do not pause enough, fill silence with noise, and they keep talking. They add fillers words such as; ums, so..., anyway, ye/yep, or use sounds including mhm, uh ha, or low grunts, when they should just be quiet; and instead use body language such as a head nod or a smile to indicate they like what the other is saying.

Overusing verbal communication can lead to unexpected and unpleasant results. You may have heard this statement used in interrogation at a courthouse or police station, "whatever you say can and will be held against you." Just as in body language, our subconscious involuntarily and automatically shoots out words. When we do not take the time to pause and use the downtime buffer to our advantage, an array of truths spews out. Any leaked truth has the potential to interfere with or bring unsuccessful results in our life. Our listeners can use these truths to manipulate or for judgement over and over again.

Overusing is simply the noise of useless words that many often throw away in an attempt to gain attention, appear smart, friendly or popular. Ironically, the more we talk, the less we are able to communicate, as this creates a thick fog of information overload that makes it really difficult to actually understand each other; and if we do not apply the practice of listening we miss out on vast number of verbal signals that can assist in attaining successful results.

Pausing gives listeners' time to process what we are saying, and the opportunity to respond or ask questions if they are unclear of our speech, this is also applies to us as the listener.

We are subconsciously wired more as emotional beings and less as a thinking being. When we communicate with another, we must connect with them on an emotional level, more so than an intellectual level. This means simplifying the content to only what is relevant and reducing our emotions in order to focus on emotions to suit the listener. You can do this by consciously holding back unnecessary emotions, the ones that do not apply to your present interaction such as unrelated worries or anxiety, instead focus on the ones that matter the most in the NOW, current interaction.

Here are examples to assist you along your path to success:

Think Before You Speak

Many have heard the above title, yet it is so underused, we often speak before we think. Our conditioned beliefs have created impulses for 'taking the stage,' or holding a conversation is good communication, and silence is rude, or there is something wrong with someone if they are not speaking. What rubbish! We often open our mouth without really knowing what we are going to say. Sometimes we improvise, and it may come out right, however most of the time, it is random or useless topics, without any quality for contribution to the conversation or positive increase for ourselves and another, such as; the news, weather, gossip or what another has done to us. What we as an individual have experienced often has no relevance to the listener, it is only venting or complaining; the important aspect of this low quality information is that our as well as their subconscious is listening, and preparing to give us more crappy results.

Pause and take a breath before you add more words to a conversation or respond to what is being said, no matter how urgent an answer or statement may appear. Think about the words and frequency before you express, because response has many options, not just one. Ponder the relevance to any of your or others verbal communication, anything well thought can only lead to a successful outcome and people will be more responsive to listen.

Listen Before Jumping To Conclusions

The need for speed in our current existence such as the internet and consumerism has affected us in subconscious ways and this sense of urgency has flowed into our interactions. Often, we force our interactions by reaching conclusions as quick as possible, based on just one gesture, a few words, or a few sentences. We create a perspective of some thing or someone, which may be inaccurate because we did not take the opportunity to pause or to actually listen.

Listening not only means to give another time to finish their speech, it is also the exercise of borrowing their perspective, in other words to see it through their eyes and from their point of view.

What is Important

This applies to common statement, 'information overload' Communication is not about the quantity of information available to us, whether we are smart, resourceful or friendly. Communication is about the relevance of our information.

Have you ever contemplated about what to say and is it really that important?

Silence really IS gold. Sometimes we communicate just to hear the sound of our voice, regardless if we do this out loud, by writing emails or posting on Facebook. Imagine if you embraced silence, how much truth you would learn and how great your interactions could be because you focussed only on what is really important and relevant.

Every time we open your mouth to verbally communicate, we add more fog to information overload and our body language goes into overdrive. Everyone already has a massive amount of information stored in their subconscious mind, why add anything that does not aid another in positive increase. If your lounge room is full, would you keep adding more things until it is so cluttered that you don't know where to sit or are too overwhelmed to find anything, little only clean it.

Letting go of irrelevance is letting go of things that have negative connections or serve no worthwhile purpose. This makes space for positive replacements. Cluttered thoughts can make people feel disorganised, uncreative, tired, anxious and burdened. This clutter blocks or fogs the mind, becomes stagnate and then transmutes to negative energy.

In order to get new successful results in your life you have to release old things. You can even apply this to the clutter within your own mind. Omit everything that does not give you outcomes you desire by letting go of everything from your previous experiences that did not work out for you such as; failure, relationship problems, financial problems. Previous experiences also mean yesterday or an hour ago.

When clutter resides or is absorbed by the subconscious mind it acts to deliver chaos. Chaos in mixed body language as well as speech.

By holding onto any thoughts, emotions or beliefs that are not pleasant we hold onto old energy patterns that block our path to success, and we indicate to the subconscious that we are not ready to move forward to our desired future because we prefer the results we have. Even holding onto these for a later date, or as a 'just in case' is indicating we want to invite more of the already experienced adversity to come back another time/s.

Baggage from old relationships such as the ex-cheated, ripped you off, or burnt you in some way, plays no part in the NOW, interactions. Nor does what happened to your car, friend, family member, financial situation and so on. Allowing these emotions of past experiences to reside within us spills over during our interactions and expresses as our body language. Even when people in our presence are not doing horrible things to us we show indications of mistrust, doubt, or expressions where we expect the worse to happen, and this can create an unpleasant result. If you carry all that old clutter into your interactions, there is no room in your life for new things to prosper. Success will pass you by because you're too busy holding on to the clutter of a non-existent past.

Get To Know Others

Do things together, not only talk about things together. Silently watch the sunset together, play a game, go for a walk or have a meal. All these are actions that apart from the main benefit of enjoying life, also have a secondary, very important outcome; they help you understand others better.

Create a Better Reality

When we speak less, we do more, our focus switches from talking to doing. Doing includes listening, learning, bonding, assisting and resting your own active mind. If we refrained from talking for only ten minutes a day for thirty days this would account to five hours a month. What would you do with this time? Whatever you want, of course. Or perhaps getting to know your inner workings from what you have learned from listening, so that you can transmute your patterns for a desired life.

Try this:

When in a conversation speak for only three minutes then pause for longer, listen to others around you, observe their body language, speech, tone of voice and the environment. There is much that can be said in three minutes, and you get the opportunity to speak again, only every time you do, pause for with silent intervals. Studies have shown that people don't remember much of what they hear when communicating, yet, with less speech recall improves. Therefore, whatever you say in the three minutes is genuinely heard, so make it memorable.

Deception Detection

On an average sixty-seven percent of accuracy is found when detecting the truth, whereas forty-four percent is found while detecting deception. Our accuracy at detecting truth is higher than our accuracy at detecting lies. While lying is common, we more so expect people to be honest and are therefore better at detecting truth instead of a lie. Seeking truth is inherent within us and this is why we negate the possibility of another's deception. Also, due to our subconscious fears, we feel it would be detrimental to act suspiciously while speaking with others just in case they were telling the truth.

Lies leak through causing the body to freeze up and lock down as a fear response. Truth projects as worry free, a loose body and presents more hand and arm emphatic gestures. When observing half-hearted attempts such as lack of emphasis with gestures, this indicates a story is fabricated. Truth tellers emphasise gestures to set facts straight and will go to lengths to accomplish this.

When someone is guilty they harbour negative thoughts, they find it difficult to achieve comfort because by nature, people are honest and believe themselves to be good people. This is true, as none of us are born bad, it is only the beliefs we learned from our environments that automatically affects how we express to others.

When examining someone for truth we must be mindful that false positives are not produced. This means that people who are actually innocent will plead guilty. Innocent suspects have confessed to serious crimes such as murder simply because they were put under intense pressure. This is why it is imperative that we establish comfort during all interactions, avoid interrogation and use appropriate questions to uncover the truth. Our body language should present as neutral and remain calm whilst the information, details, asking for clarification, and so on is relayed in order to uncover the discomfort.

Guide to Comfort/Discomfort

COMFORT

People will signal comfort in various ways, and our goal is to look for patterns in the signals. When someone is truly comfortable, they will express multiple "Comfort" body language cues. Here are some common key comfort signals that are easy to spot;

Moving Closer, Leaning In, or Face to Face

When someone is comfortable with another or interested in the conversation, they shrink physical distance. If someone FEELS close to you, they want to BE close to you.

Shrinking distance can express as; leaning towards another, turn to face another, or physically moving closer. An object or obstruction can be moved that is between the participants such as, pushing the dinner plate aside at a restaurant. Feet in particular are a reliable indicator. Someone might consciously face towards another, yet they are unaware of what their feet are doing. Feet pointed towards another, is a genuine expression of comfort and therefore a very good signal.

Head Tilted or Rested upon a Hand

A tilted head indicates curiosity, whereas resting their head on their hand implies that someone is intently listening. Both indicate comfort. If someone is focused on what is being verbally expressed, it is common for them to lean forward, rest the elbow on a table and the head upon the hand.

Leg Tuck

When a female is sitting beside someone they are comfortable with, they often tuck one leg beneath the buttocks or other leg and turn towards that person. The receiver can count themselves lucky as it indicates that someone enjoys their company.

Subtle Smile

Generally, people do not grin madly throughout an encounter, and if they do this indicates underhanded thoughts. When people are enjoying themselves, often the corners of their mouth will be turned up slightly. And though it is subtle it indicates one feels joy from the circumstance and people/person around them.

Physical Touch

This is a significant indicator of comfort. If someone is feeling comfortable with you, they are likely to touch your shoulder, put their hand on your knee, or give you a hug when they greet you. Physical touch varies by individuals, if someone is not touching they may not be a touchy type or it could be a cultural mannerism.

DISCOMFORT

Alike many signals, discomfort expressions appear in patterns, and are best understood in context. When a discomfort signal presents, you can take action to alter the situation. Pattern interrupts can be used for discomfort signals to help ease interactions. Here are some common key discomfort signals that are easy to spot;

Neck Touching or Rubbing

The neck is home to many nerve endings that, when rubbed, will lower heart rate and create comfort. When someone is uncomfortable, they automatically and unconsciously touch the neck. This is a natural inherent response in order for the nerve endings to activate and help to calm the mind and body. Rubbing or stroking the front or back of the neck is the most common discomfort expression, however, fiddling with a necklace or a necktie, also indicates discomfort.

Face Touching or Rubbing

Our face also has nerve endings therefore people will rub their face to ease discomfort and calm themselves down. This can express as; rubbing the forehead, eyes, lips, playing with the hair, puffing out cheeks and exhaling.

Leg Rubbing

This is where a seated person places hands (or hand), palm-down upon leg/s and slide the palm towards the knee/s, much like wiping off sweaty palms.

Withdrawing or Blocking

When in conversation, and someone becomes uncomfortable, they pull back, lean away or place objects between them and another. They may adjust the chair so that they are not facing the person directly or may cross arms to block their chest and/or cross their legs to block another with the knee. Be mindful and consider context when observing withdrawing or blocking. Sometimes people may cross legs or lean back to sit more comfortably, or cross arms because they are cold.

Feet Pointed Away

Feet are powerful indicators of actual feelings and thoughts. Feet pointed away from a conversation whether someone is seated or standing indicates a desire to exit the conversation. .

Interrupting Hand

This is not a signal of discomfort so much as an indication that another wants to communicate verbally. When someone wants to speak, the hand interrupts with signals such as; a jerk upwards or pointer finger raised. The hand will only raise partway before stopping, this indicates that the person wants to interject, but they stopped themselves before saying anything.

Eye Contact

Nobody maintains eye contact at all times, however when someone looks away they should soon look back to you. If someone is looking everywhere but you, this indicates discomfort. When someone repeatedly looks away at one specific thing. For instance, when another is talking they keep glancing over their shoulder at someone else, shows that they would rather talk to that person. A way of determining discomfort is to say the person's name in the conversation. For example, "Isn't that right, John?" Upon hearing their name, people will look at you and hold eye contact for several moments. If someone glances when you say their name, then immediately look away, this is a definite signal for discomfort.

Acting on Discomfort Signals

Focusing on comfort and discomfort can be easier than trying to memorise every signal in body language (and there are hundreds). Here is an exercise that will assist you by observing body language in portions for easy memorisation.

Choose one or two signals from the list:

<u>Comfort</u>
Moving Closer, Leaning In, or Face to Face
Head Tilted or Rested upon a Hand
Leg Tuck

Subtle Smile

Physical Touch

Discomfort

Face Touching or Rubbing

Leg Rubbing

Withdrawing or Blocking

Feet Pointed Away

Interrupting Hand

Eye Contact

Now practice observing the one or two signals:
1. On the television or via your computer find a live-action show that has a lot of social interaction such as Reality TV which has mostly talking.
2. Look for the signal/s you selected. If you are able, rewind a scene so that you can observe expressions closely and thoroughly. Keep practicing until you are satisfied and feel you are able to notice these signal/s in a physical interaction.
3. Now that you can recognise the selected signal/s choose a few more and work your way through the list.

You can even apply this practice to yourself, so you can notice your own body language when interacting with others.

With a little practice, awareness of body language is easier to notice and becomes second nature. However, it's not enough to just know when someone is uncomfortable we also need to take action to make them comfortable. Once you decipher the pattern of signals you can alter the circumstance with a pattern interrupt, then follow this with a way that aids in harmonising the interaction.

Chapter 7
Your Body Language

If you detect a body language that signals someone is uncomfortable, you now know to look for the cause of their discomfort and then try to alter it. If someone signals that they are feeling comfortable, you know that you can relax and enjoy the interaction. But how do people interpret the body language signals that you give?

It's true that only a few people have trained themselves to consciously analyse body language. But even when conversing with another that does not consciously think about your body language, they will still subconsciously react to it. For example, if your body language expresses warmth and friendliness, another is likely to sense this and relax. If your body language demonstrates disinterest or boredom, another will think twice before sharing something personal with you. The subconscious mind and intuition is constructed as a beacon to always be attentive to signals from the outer environment, most are not aware of this, because they have not practiced listening to their inner self.

Beacon Body

"There is a way that nature speaks, that land speaks (our body). Most of the time we are simply not patient enough, quiet enough, to pay attention to the story." - *Linda Hogan*

Much like a lighthouse is the watchtower for the seafarers, which guides and informs of risk, our beacons are the watchtower for our physical, emotional, and mental bodies.

We are an incredible help to ourselves because we are gifted with self-navigational instincts. These are indicated by our mental faculties (capabilities of the mind). Our way to feel through and choose what truly feels goods for our personal experiences. These are;

Instinct: We HAVE stimulus in the mind that produces a definite change of momentum. Unconditioned response. An urge that incites, rouses, encourages, and stimulates us to act.

Reasoning: We CAN question, argue and challenge. Just remember, to consider when reasoning, are you doing this from your unique self, or conditioned self.

Intuition: We HAVE the ability to understand something instinctively, without the need for reasoning. Our sensations, our beacons are our insight, direct or immediate cognition, and our spiritual perception.

Perception: We CAN interpret, regard or understand something. And recognize any 'something' how we choose to interpret or believe it, with or without influence and conditioned beliefs.

Memory: We HAVE a mind that stores and remembers information, cares, and thinks. We are not limited to conditioned thoughts only, within us resides the knowledge of the Universe and this is our true memory.

Creation: WE ARE THE CREATOR of our experience, and we are the triggers for thought to come into being, to create and produce a thing, sensation or experience.

Will: We CAN express a strong intention and certainty; with no doubt and resolution. We CAN live on purpose for our desires. We request and command our outcomes. And we are fearless.

Imagination: We HAVE unconditional and unlimited thought, always, anywhere, anytime and endless.

Choice: We CAN choose between two or more unlimited possibilities and invent some through our imagination.

Intention: We CAN live on purpose and deliberately choose, aim or plan our desires.

Of all our beacons intuition is the greater for guidance. It is the inner voice, a hunch, a thought or sensation which says, "this is the way". A better description for intuition would be 'our spiritual faculty' that is above intellectual understanding. It is a magic path and sense that watches over us and never sleeps. Nothing is irrelevant with intuition because it guides us in the yay or nay of our next step. Intuition has the power of eternal youth and eternal life because when follow our unique bliss we bring into our experience happiness and a physiology of ideal health.

We began this physical life experience exposed to and educated by only conditioned beliefs. We had to start somewhere! From here, right now, we can learn from and gain insights from that which we do not want and change them into what we desire. We could never have known what we wanted had we not experienced the unwanted, because comparisons give us a deeper understanding.

Our intellectual understanding has taught us to reason through our conditioned beliefs, and sometimes it takes practice to notice only our intuition. The practice of tuning into intuition is a must and an important part of development in understanding body language, because this is the straight line and shortest route to confirmation of truth.

Begin to listen to your body. We all have the ability to assess what is right or wrong, what feels good or bad. When you are feeling good this is your inner message or intuition indicating something positive. Take advice from your inner guidance.

Notice your sensations: When a sensation feels light, warm or tingly, particularly around the chest area, this is your intuition indicating that all is well. If you feel discomfort, a sickly feeling, tension or tightness around the stomach/solar plexus area, your intuition is alerting you about something unpleasant or risk.

When in doubt, trust your instinct, the sensations, it can be your saviour when you are unable to pinpoint specific cues. Stay focussed on what is before you. Focus can unclutter the mind and you will be more than just a passive observer, you become an active observer with a clearer mind to tap into your inner guidance.

"You have the Answer. Just get quiet enough to hear it." - *Pat Obuchowski*

When Your Body Language And Your Words Don't Coordinate

Most people do not think about their own body language instead more effort goes into thinking of perfect words to say, yet they are unaware that their body language and their words are sending very different messages. For example, say you have had a long, hard day, but a friend wants to talk about something they are struggling with. You obviously care about your friend, so you agree to talk. If during the conversation you are yawning, looking at the clock, and leaning back in your chair with your arms crossed, your friend might conclude that you do not care about what they have to say, or you had no interest in talking in the first place. They storm off, and you are left wondering what you said wrong. You said nothing wrong---your body expressions did!

There are numerous examples as to how your own body language can create misunderstandings. When your words and body are uncoordinated, people will tend to go with the message that your body is sending.

Magic of Self-Awareness

Fortunately, unintended messages are avoidable when we are aware of the patterns our body is expressing. Our bodies will always communicate, it is part of being human.

We just require to nurture ourselves by taking the time to notice what our body communicates involuntarily and automatically, this way we can ensure we transmute our body language to match the words we verbally communicate.

It is important when changing your body gestures that you do this authentically, and not use this language to mask deception. If your words are communicating something untrue, change your words instead of your body language, your body is the honest of the two. Relationships built on deception will never give long-term satisfaction, nor will it be of any benefit to you, it will only bring about stress, concern and ill health.

When we are aware of something is has less power over us, therefore recognition is the first step in changing automatic body language.
Here are some ways that were mentioned in an earlier chapter to assist you, even stop your automatic body language:
- Tune in and observe your body's conversational movements. When you recognise some patterns that relay undesired messages, consciously alter your own body language, to suit the verbal conversation. This also grants you the opportunity to let go of the subconscious imprints that don't give you the results that you want.

- Practice in the mirror. This can reveal how your body language expresses. By watching your reflection, you can pick up on automatic language. Particularly your facial gestures. Talk to yourself, such as; "Look how happy you are" or "you're super smart and popular". Does your subconscious mind believe you? Watch what your hidden thoughts signal. Do your eyes look away, this indicates discomfort. Are you blinking more, this indicates inner struggle. Are you exhaling this indicates easing the discomfort. What are your eyebrows, mouth, even feet and hands doing? These too can signal what your true feelings are.

- The best way to discover your automatic body language is to watch a video recording of yourself. Watch your body language and gestures. See if they match the words you are saying. This is very much an eye opener for anyone and you get to see what others see. It can be quite confronting, but don't let this stop you. Move forward in observing yourself, this way you get to see your involuntary expressions, and with this recognition you can alter projections that are undesirable or serve no purpose for you.

-

- Another way is to listen to, not ask, what others say to you, about you. These patterns seen by others can unveil clues to your unrecognised habits.
-

Remember... Any imprint was instilled at a previous time, the past. The past is nothing but ether, blank air now. It's only the memories we give power to that keep interfering in our path to success. This now non-existent past has no place in giving you the results you desire. This is impossible, because you are not that child or teenager any longer. Nor are you that employee, partner or title of former experiences. You right NOW are in a new phase of your life because you only exist in a place called NOW, not yesterday and YOU CAN choose to create very different memories.

Focus on presenting united, genuine messages that are both true and relates to another. If you are tired yet, you care about a friend who is sitting before you, the most important expression is "I care about you" not "I'm tired" (even though both messages are true.) If you are excited to meet someone new but also nervous, the message that is most important is "I am excited to meet you" not "I am nervous." Prioritising an expression is good practice when we mean multiple things at once. This is not deception, it is empathic consideration, which often results in positive outcomes.

Take the time to be aware of your own body language. Start with observing your comfort and discomfort signals. When you notice a discomfort, cue make the effort to transmute this signal, action a pattern interrupt so that you may broadcast comfort signals. Take advantage of the downtime buffer to process your next step. You'll find that as you match your body language to your words, you will have much greater success in your interactions.

Authenticity To Yourself and Others

Know thyself and "To thine own self be true!" what does it mean to be true to yourself, an authentic person, or someone who is genuine? Authenticity is often defined as an absence of pretence with words and behaviours by being true and honest with oneself and to others.

Becoming authentic is an individual mission, since each person has their own way of being human, therefore, authentic expression will be different for each individual. The unique nature of an individual is best seen by not who they are, but in who they become, and becoming authentic is a continuous process, not an event. It involves not just knowing thyself, but also having an awareness of others so that they too can experience fulfilment.

Many people know that it is good to listen to yourself as this can indicate how we are feeling. However, another very powerful process is to talk to oneself, because sometimes you need to speak truth to yourself. Your thoughts and emotions always speak in silence, they may say that you stuffed up, you are angry or that nothing matters. There is a way to counteract this. It is YOU verbally conversing with YOU. What can you outwardly say to yourself? This can be a reminder of people who love you and all of the good things in your life. This edification is a pattern interrupt to raise positive emotions.

Anxiety has a way of filling our thoughts with rubbish. It can imply that terrible things will happen if we try to accomplish our goals, such as doing something different or going on a long road trip. The patterned behavioural thinking takes over known as, 'what if' or 'what if, down' Verbal speech interrupts the mind, and this is because thinking and speaking do not work well together. Therefore, when we speak, we put a cone of silence over the thoughts and hear only our outer voice. When negative thoughts present start conversing with yourself, you can tell yourself that your fear is lying to you, or change the patterned thinking to, 'what if, up'. What if… things do turn out well?

Self-Honesty

You are an incredible, brave, beautiful person, and life holds so much promise for you. Do not allow fear, depression, loneliness or anger blind you to the truth of who you are. You have done many wonderful things so far, if you reflect back through your life you would remember them, you can even recall some experiences that had great times.

It really does feel good when someone has something nice to say about us. Yet, most neglect to say something nice to themselves. Feeling good about a compliment works in both ways, whether by another or from ourself. There really is a lot you can admire about yourself. For example: you cooked a great meal, someone smiled because of you, you can see beauty in certain things, and you exist because it was meant to be, this is why your future holds possibilities, everyone and everything has a purpose, yours is unfolding. The world as a whole is balanced because you are here and is looking forward to whatever you create.

You can speak truth to another, too.
Remind them that you care and tell them about the greatness you see in them. Tell them that you are gracious to have them in your life, and that this matters to you. A reminder is a breath of fresh air, and gift you can offer anytime. And don't

be afraid to ask for this gift in return. If you feel weighed down, ask another to talk with you. There are approximately 7.6 billion people on our planet, with this amount we all belong somewhere and with someone/s.

Bulls#*t Fear

Fear is simply a clever ambush, an invention created in the imagination that declines our confidence and gives to us ill health and unwanted outcomes from the unique frequencies of anxiety and stress. Fear is an unpleasant stream of thoughts that are fuelled by conditioned beliefs. Beliefs of 'what if… downs' and 'just in case'; the must do or not do something that lives in the future and not in our present moment. They are not real, and only become our outcomes if we willingly hand over our creative power to our conditioned thoughts that hold bulls#*t illusions of safety. Illusions shared to us by the media, news, family and environmental customs. Many of these beliefs were purely created to benefit the ones who created them, so that we may, buy, action or become the servant or follower to someone or something; and to help veil their insecurities so that they can pretend to be a superior. Do not view fear as bad though, this is simply another sensation from our beacon and it just 'IS'. The 'IS' has no meaning, fear is actually fear-less and only becoming something to fear when we attach a definition to it.

The Vibrational Body

This and the following title contain excerpts from my book' *Festival of the Imagination.*

Our physical bodies are secondary to our energy body. Any disruption in the flow of this energy pattern results in deterioration and dis-ease to the physical body. It is our minds state which governs the frequency such as; happy or sad, confused or peaceful, because we accept these as beliefs. Our emotional state, and our beacon (our lighthouse), will signal us of our minds state (our thoughts); and both will guide us either to keep going in the right direction with pleasant emotions; or our beacon will blow a horn informing us of the risk, such as a headache, discomfort, sadness or anger, alerting us to divert our thinking to something else.

Emotions along with thoughts, solid objects, people, animals, plants and everything else is made up of matter (energy, substance or content). Or as Wallace Wattles wrote in his book, *'The Science of Getting Rich'*- *"A thinking stuff that forms all things."*

All physical and non-physical matter is composed of vibration, the same energy that resides within us. This vibrational frequency is different in everything, the frequency is determined by the number of components, such as; number of atoms, molecules, protons, neurons, or electrons. There are boundless combinations, and each vary, no two are identical and each are the results in the physical and non-physical realms. For example, no two leaves, people, flowers, cups, animals or chairs are the same in matter, each has its own unique energetic frequency that support their particular existence.

The Universal Law of Vibration states: Everything in the universe is energy. It is ever moving, vibrating at different frequencies, and always shifting into various forms. These vibrations vary. Each of us are energy vibrating at a specific frequency.

Our minds are a vibrating force and every thought, including beliefs, is matter, vibrating at a specific frequency. Whatever frequency we hold we will match *"the thinking stuff that forms all things,"* and bring it into our physical experience. We are a 'thinking Creator'.

What is labelled as positive emotions such as love, happy, calm, joy or serenity is correlated to high or fast moving vibrational frequency. This is because these frequencies show signs of wellness, vibrancy, vitality and all that gives to us 'feel good' experiences. Lower or slower vibrational frequencies are what brings to us negative emotional states such as illness, depression, anger or lack of vitality.

In the previous paragraph I began with 'What is labelled.' This is because it is not the word, nor is it an emotion. We give emotions titles so that we may recognise them, and this serves as another tool in our creating. Each emotion is purely a unique vibration and the frequency pattern, or the composition of its matter gives us the unique sensation. The sensation of the frequency.

The energy matrix of any experience is reliant upon a certain frequency of vibration. It cannot exist if it has no frequency and we cannot have an experience without matching the thought to the frequency. When we alter our vibrational frequency, we directly affect our physical world. Therefore, if there are unwanted experiences, events, thoughts, sensations, or conditioned beliefs we only just need change our thoughts.

Transformation (change the form of) requires practice. A practise that is alien and conflicting to our conditioned habits. If it were not unusual and conflicting, then everyone would already have transformed and have their desired outcomes. Our conditioned habits keep us in a dreamlike state, where we feel that a desired result is hard work or impossible to attain because of…….. You can fill the gap, if you choose. There is an array of excuses, from negative conditioned thoughts, and it is not worth the read. And it's just a bad, ridiculous dream.

Transmute Energy

If you don't like the dream you're in, wake up. Change the sheets and move the bed to another position. Transforming unwanted conditioned habits is no different to changing the sheets and moving a bed. Awareness is to recognise the conditioned patterns when they interfere with your practises and at these moments you can dismiss the intruder who entered without permission. You are in control and give permission for entry into your experience, not your conditioned thoughts. We all must adopt a practise and change the form of our patterns to new conditioned patterns that are suitable and matching in frequency to our desired results.

When a frequency vibration accelerates it results to a higher vibrational frequency, higher feel good sensations and this can be achieved with ease. The faster we expand our mind with these high vibrational frequencies we place ourselves in more feel-good sensations increasing our inner happiness and serenity. Here are three ways we can do this:

The first is meditation! The word meditation is from *meditationem,* "a thinking over, reflect, consider." However, though this word is very much used as the term for going within, there is another term that is more suitable to this definition. Because, when we go within we free ourselves to; examine from within, look into, and observe our self and only our authentic self, in the quiet of our mind, without the noise (sound and objects) of the outside world. This word is, Introspection.

We must have moments to calm our thoughts. We live in an active world of technology, attitudes, daily tasks, general living, conditioned thoughts and an influx of body language gestures and verbal communication. This is Self-Knowledge practice and is <u>the most powerful</u> way to alter vibration and raise vibrational frequency. We enter introspection with movement of breath.

The breath is the conductor of life force energy. Breathing through the nose and out through the mouth allows us to calm, and alters mind and body vibration, raising vibrational frequency. The higher the frequency, the more unloaded we feel in our physical, emotional, and mental bodies. We unblock, release and unclutter our mind and bodies; and create greater clarity for unencumbered power to return. Uninterrupted energy flow. As Bashar stated: *"You cannot see the forest for the trees unless you are outside the forest."* We need to be outside the forest, the clutter to be in a position to know, see and our patterns, and choose what our unique self (authentic, inner self) wants, without conditional views impeding us.

Our breath is the way we connect the mental state with the physical body, it is also another tool in understanding our emotional thoughts (sensations) at any moment. Thoughts and sensations affect our breathing patterns and these patterns are indicators for controlling our experience. A calm breath is our indication of high vibration, of being in a peaceful state. Heavier, quick breaths indicate unease and this will create our unwanted experiences including ill health.

Breath is not only our conductor of life force energy; it is also a tool to reset frequency anytime. Take a deep breath through your nose, hold it for a moment then release it from your mouth. Interrupt the frequency if you do not feel good and reclaim your power in any given moment. Let your breath be a reset and do this as many times as you require until you feel and hear the calmness of your breath.

Going within or inward influences our physical, emotional, and mental bodies, rewarding us with wellness, tranquility, and an inner happiness that can only be experienced because words are not enough to describe the totality of this experience; and introspection invites more like frequency to keep flowing into our experience. It also amplifies clarity, and this gives opportunity for us to have dominion over the conditioned thoughts and beliefs because the clutter dissolves. And introspection (meditation) is the place where you can hear the answer of your own heart, your soul's voice.

There are many ways to enter introspection. We can listen to a guided meditation, place soft, calming music on, or have a completely quiet space. You can use candles, oils or crystals if you wish. These, as well as calming music, all have unique frequencies and will add a successful result. We can sit, lay, head on pillow or not, there is no one way, only the way in which you feel comfort. Begin this practice with arms and legs unfolded, as folded limbs impede the free flow of energy, and inhale through the nose, hold for a few seconds, then exhale out of your mouth, simply focus on the breath and this will begin the process of calm frequency. A helpful way to cancel out any distractions, from mind or external sounds is to count the seconds of breath. For example; inhale on the count of three, hold for two seconds and exhale on the count of five, releasing any unwanted frequencies held within your physical body. Just focus on your breath, wander deeper into a relaxed state and allow whatever enters the mind to flow naturally. There is no one way for this either; colours, one colour, faces, ideas or personal thoughts may enter the mind, it is your own unique experience.

Getting to know our unique self (authentic, inner self) is the greatest occupation we can volunteer to our self. We can pursue and attain many things in life, believing an event or item will make us happy, however, when we receive these 'things' we are not as happy as we thought we would be, the novelty and excitement washes away within days, weeks or months and we are back to pursuing another yearning. How satisfied we are with the decisions we make is a measure of how well we know our true self. When we give our self-quiet time to get in touch with our soul voice and go within, we gain clarity and insight into what it is that we uniquely desire. These unique desires are the ones that give us bountiful happiness with lasting results. And the novelty will never wear off.

There are many things in life that are achieved through activity, however, our souls voice is one that comes to us when we stop activity, reflect upon our experiences, and connect to our unique self. We must give ourselves time to rest, recover and recharge. To go within is more refreshing than a deep night's sleep. It is a watchful and relaxed reset. A reset from the conditional thoughts to unconditional unique thoughts.

The second tool we can use to expand our mind to high vibrational frequencies is by music or sound. These each have a unique frequency to accelerate vibration:

Music: classical music such as Baroque enhances concentration. 528Hz tones and music, this is known as the miracle or love frequency and can be found on the internet. Soft calming music, such as natural sounds of water or birds also has high vibrational frequency.

Sound: audios containing music and speech of hypnosis and paraliminals. These are a process of induced suggestion. We have already experienced induced suggestions through repetition experienced from our environments, such as media, our families and school days, this is why we have conditioned beliefs. These audios induce new conditionings and we can choose the specific outcomes we desire. There are many to choose from here are some examples; health improvement, reverse aging, increase happiness, forgiveness, stop procrastination, intuition amplifiers or wealth mindset enhancement. These can be found on the internet as well.

The third vibration accelerator is Feng Shui. A science and ancient art based on laws for energy flow. This is practised through formulas and calculations using energy forces referred to as Qi (chi). Both Feng and Shui are associated with good health and prosperity. If energy in the environment remains stuck, people are prevented from moving forward, or may experience unwanted occurrences, however, by increasing the flow of energy this clears the path to propel us forward and to bring to fruition desired intentions. When changes are created in the environment it produces advancement and enhancement in the level and flow of Qi energy.

Our environment is our physical visualisation board, and this unconsciously creates our outcomes, as well as our body language, all day, every day. Just as everything is energy, our environment is energy and everything within it has its own unique vibration.

Feng Shui teaches that our external environment will always reflect our internal environment. When we shift or change our outer environment this becomes an energetic shifter to the inner self, the mind. If we align our physical environment with our desires this enables us to direct our lives, to change our experience and have command with how we choose our life experiences to be.

Look closely at your environment and observe what it is telling you. Can you see the reflection of your results? Can you see what is or is not happening in your life? Are there any objects or images that reflect a sad or angry life? Is there clutter? If there is clutter, this will add clutter to the mind. Think of clutter as not just a clutter of items, but rather as a clutter of energies.

It is essential for mental clarity and focus to create an environment, or simply a room with less furniture and fewer things that require tending to. When we have fewer distractions, we have stronger concentration and stay focused on our goals, it improves our motivation and energy flow. Look about, is there anything you can remove, donate or sell that will aide in calming your thoughts? Take action, clear out unwanted energy clutter and make room for more possibilities from your imagination.

For many years I put a lot of work and effort into expanding my life to success. I had heard about Feng Shui over the years, yet I brushed it off as one of those hippie things. It was not until I studied and mastered this all-important science of energy flow and applied it to my life that I realised all along there was something that could help take some of the pressure off attaining my life's desires. Feng Shui is my assistant that helps results come to me with ease and very little effort. You too can study this or appoint a Feng Shui Consultant to help activate your environment in being conducive to attaining the life results you want.

For more information about what is involved with Feng Shui you can go to: **http://www.terminafengshui.com/**
Or
To obtain easy to follow guides in activating your environment for desired results, you can find these books at:
 https://www.perpelflame.com/shop

Chapter 8
Interpret Facial Expressions

Numerous studies have been carried out in regard to facial expressions and the importance of this body expression. Not only does it reveal hidden thoughts and feelings of others, the studies discovered that people make judgments in regard to level of intelligence based upon faces and the expressions such as; individuals with a narrow face and prominent nose are perceived as intelligent. People with smiling, joyful expression are also judged as being more intelligent than those with angry expressions.

Eyes have been shown through these studies to be more reliable than other body language expressions. Charles Darwin stated that *"most people do not bother to censor their body movements",* instead people make a conscious attempt to control their facial expressions. Regardless of the pretend attempts with facial features, the eyes tell a different story. This is because the movements eyes make are involuntary and sudden. There is a lot revealed about what a person is thinking just by how the eyes move.

Eyes are an important indicator, yet all facial gestures can reveal our true hidden feelings about another or of a particular situation such as; a smile can indicate approval or happiness. A frown can signal disapproval or unhappiness. Some examples of emotions that can be expressed with facial expressions include: Happiness, Sadness, Anger, Surprise, Disgust, Fear, Confusion, Excitement, Desire, Contempt and Pain. Facial expressions can even help to determine if we should trust or believe what another is verbalising. For example; a trustworthy facial expression expresses as a slight raise of the eyebrows and a slight smile, this indicates both friendliness and confidence.

Eyes

The eyes are frequently referred to as the "windows to the soul" and can reveal a great deal about what the 'soul' (the energy body) is feeling or thinking. When asked a question eyes look straight ahead to consider an answer, indicating a passive consideration. Eyes looking down indicates that someone is concentrating or evaluating, and eyes looking upward signals that an idea is being evaluated. During a conversation, eyes looking off into space indicates a loss of interest, and avoidance of eye contact indicates submission, discomfort or fear.

Results of research have discovered that approximately sixty percent of conversation involved some form of gazing. This includes thirty percent is mutual gazing where the eyes meet and eye contact is held directly. The remaining percentage includes; looking twice at something or someone while listening or speaking to another. The average gaze lasts about three seconds whereas a mutual gaze lasts only just over one second before being broken.

Eye gazing is also an indication of speech patterns. People often look away as they begin to speak to avoid distraction and return the gaze once the thought is clear for verbal delivery. Eye contact can be used to measure like-mindedness. When more agreement emerges, more eye contact is present, indicating acceptance, 'I like you'. Yet, if someone holds eye contact for extended period of time, the response will also result in another expressing acceptance and a sense of 'like'.

When interacting with others, observe eye movements such as whether someone has direct eye contact or are averting their gaze, how much they are blinking, or if their pupils are dilated. We tend to sense in distrust others who express poor eye contact because our inherent subconscious belief responds in saying they are hiding something. Here are some examples to aid in understanding eye language:

Eye gaze

When someone looks directly into your eyes during a conversation, it indicates that they are interested and paying attention. However, prolonged eye contact can feel threatening. Breaking eye contact and frequently looking away can indicate that the person is distracted, uncomfortable, or trying to conceal real feelings.

Affectionate people will alter a position and bring eyes to level of another, whereas, those that are less affectionate lean forward and use gaze less frequently. These are expressions we experienced from our early development, our childhood and because of this we have formulated our patterns which present as automatic, involuntary body language. Only with conscious effort can we change them, but first, we must understand the purpose and function of gaze and also what good gaze habits really are.

Eye Gaze is different to a stare. Stares are daggers, shooting invisible arrows into the face of another. Gaze reveals cues that signal interest, attention, affiliation, intimacy, approval, dominance, aggression, openness and desired personal involvement. A gaze invites and expresses warmth, it indicates positive emotions and connection.

The language of gazing presents in various ways, such as; the face-gaze- when one person directs their eyes at another's face, the eye-gaze, when the gaze is directed toward the eyes of another that does not reciprocate or a mutual-gaze where two people look at each other's faces and this can include looking directly into each other's eyes. Other forms of gaze include omission, where someone fails to look at another without intending to do so, avoidance, where someone purposely prevents eye contact and staring, a persistent look that occurs regardless of what another is doing.

Mutual gaze is considered as a positive gesture, however the stare and eye gaze, presents as negative gestures. Prolonged eye contact when first meeting others is always taken negatively, or with hostility, and can be perceived as offensive. Prolonged eye contact can be a result of projected dislike or, disapproval of others, even when affection or attraction is felt. Holding a gaze for three seconds longer than our usual can present as over-assertiveness and create contempt.

Blinking

Blinking adds moisture to the eye along with tears and oil that is secreted from tiny glands in the inner edge of the eyelid. Increased blinking also aids in cleaning our eyes due to the added moisture, and this in turn prepares us for sight.

Though blinking is natural, we should observe whether someone is blinking too much or too little. People often blink more rapidly when feeling distressed or uncomfortable. Infrequent blinking may indicate that a person is intentionally trying to control their eye movements. For example, a poker face blinks less frequently because they purposely attempt to appear unexcited. Blinking is also subject to mimicry. When someone speaks with excitement and increase the blink rate, others often follow and blink at a similar rate. When people mimic a high blink rate, they subconsciously perceive that they too are excited, which can move them to open body language.

A normal blink lasts only about a tenth of a second and at a rate of about six to eight blinks per minute. An extended blink can last from two to three seconds or even longer. The longer the blink the more conspicuous the message.

Studies have linked arousal with increased eye blink rate therefore blinking can occur during sexual actions as well as when someone feels attraction towards another. Blink rate will increase when someone feels under pressure, or when someone feels excited. Rapid or high eye blinks indicate an inner struggle or distress which often presents when something is not in agreement, or when one is lost for words, such as the right words to express oneself. Other times when eyes flutter include; someone is troubled with performance or an issue, befuddled, stressed or simply struggling outright. This can also present when one desires to seduce another or from outer factors such as; dry air, or something like dust in the eye. Rapid blink rate is context sensitive therefore, other body language cues are essential for correct conclusion.

The opposite of the high blink is the extended blink, keeping the eyelids closed for moments, and whether by accident or by purpose, the extended blink affects others by showing disinterest and a smug attitude. It can be perceived as arrogant and pompous particularly because it expresses as temporarily shutting out the world, including the present company, indicating what others are doing or saying is not worth the energy and thought.

Ways to create a pattern interrupt with extended blinker are; reduce your blink rate or widen your eyes as if staring and hold eye contact so that they begin to mimic you. Another method is when their eyes are closed, quickly jump to the right, left or move closer. This will startle them when the eyes reopen, and naturally create a need to hold better eye contact.

Pupil size

Pupil size can be a very subtle non-verbal signal. While light in the environment affects pupil size including dimming lights, using lamps or candles so too does a change in mindset and emotions. For example, bedroom eyes, a term used to describe the look someone gives when attracted to another. Pupils are highly expanded indicating interest or even arousal.

Pupils are affected by light, they open and close to allow more or less light and this assists in proper vision. In low light conditions the pupils will expand to allow more light in and in bright conditions, the pupils will contract to restrict the amount of light.

Pupils also respond to positive stimuli by expanding or contracting when a person sees unpleasant or uninteresting stimuli. For example, pupils expand when nude images of the opposite sex are viewed and contract when viewing same sex images. Viewing unpleasant images such as unwell children, war, or torture, contracts the pupils. Pupil dilation also corresponds with mental activity. When problem solving pupils reach maximum dilation as they near a solution.

Pupil sizes can be used when observing body language because it is reliable for signals of interest and arousal. Increased pupil size can be an indication for any positive stimuli such as food when hungry, or when one sees a potential suitor in a room. Attention to the pupil size of others can give us information about the overall state people around us are in because we are not able to consciously control the size of our pupils. Eyes dilate in response to what the brain naturally thinks, which means that pupils always automatically react to stimuli we find attractive.

Studies have shown that pupil size is related to attractiveness, and larger pupils are considered more attractive. Women during the eighteenth century placed eye drops called belladonna to cause their pupils to expand in order to gain male attention. Today, marketing does the work for us. Images are doctored to appeal to our inherent response.

Eye Blocking

This term is given to eyes that squint, shield, or are covered by the hands including other objects. Covering eyes indicates feeling threatened or dislike of something seen such as horror movie previews or ads of unwell children. Squinting indicates tight focus, this is why people with compromised vision squint to read when without their glasses. When we see things we like, our pupils dilate to allow the maximum amount of light in, but when we see something we do not like, they immediately contract. This is the same when eyelids are squinted, this reduces light to the eye, as well as bringing objects into tighter focus as a defence against attack.

Covering eyes or squinting can be observed through predictive powers. For example, while questioning someone about an argument, theft, or something that recalls unpleasant images, observe when eyes contract. This will tell you which aspects of the incident are uncomfortable.

Squinting can also flash as a micro expression in conjunction with inconsistent body language to reveal hidden feelings. For example, smiling and waving at a distance while squinting, shows poor connection and an underlying distaste for the other. Squinting when reading can indicate disagreement with the content of material and this automatically expresses without awareness. An alternative to this is eyebrows as they will lower instead of eye squinting yet indicate the same message.

Social Gaze

With a friendly gaze, eyes travel in a triangular pattern from eye to eye then to the mouth with infrequent glances at the body. This gaze is non-threatening and after mutual eye-contact both people will avert their eyes downward instead of left, right or upward. Mimicry plays a part here and the gaze can be altered by anyone present. for example; to frighten someone, break your eye contact by quickly looking up and taking a step backwards, they will reciprocate thinking something is about to fall on them. Looking down, on the other hand indicates submission whereas looking left or right can signal disinterest (or interest in something else), or a desire to withdraw from the conversation. This is also expressed as; looking past someone, with an expressionless face, and unblinking eyes, as this places importance on other things aside from the conversation at hand. People will automatically, and unconsciously express feelings and judgments based on how we use eye contact during conversation regardless of our true personalities. Indication of extreme negative thoughts and feelings presents from staring, prolonged periods of unbroken eye contact.

The Business Gaze

In business eye contact begins as soon as we engage someone, yet throughput this meeting it varies depending on who we communicate with. A ratio of eighty to ninety percent of eye contact during business communication is considered appropriate. If eye contact is less than the eighty percent this can express as disinterest. If gaze is held for too long this can create discomfort, it can also present as aggression. If too short, lack of confidence or shiftiness expresses. When someone desires to level the field in business, holding a gaze longer than normal will increase dominance.

Eye contact indicates that we have someone's attention or that we are paying attention. It is not best practice to hold eye contact for too long as it can move to staring indicating overly dominant. In business, it is important not to gaze below the neckline so as not to appear sexually interested. Most of the business gaze is spent traveling from eye to eye and down only as far as the nose. The goal of the business gaze is to show interest and intensity but omit any other indicators. To convey an even greater seriousness, the eyes should travel from eye to eye then to the forehead. Remember...keep it professional, keep all gaze around the eyes, nose and forehead.

The Intimate Gaze

Eyes will follow specific patterns across the face to form an intimate gaze. Initially the eyes will be quickly averted by looking downward rather than left or right. Looking down punctuates sexual interest and presents as sexy, coy, submissive and teasing. Looking left or right indicates that one is scanning the room and is seen as stealing a look where one either, wishes not to be caught, one is not ready to reveal their true interests, or is simply scanning the room. Stealing looks is what people who are married or in a relationship do when they notice someone attractive. They look secretly to avoid detection and paying a price for looking, these looks are for their own sake, and there is no true intention of pursuit.

When interest is mutual face scanning takes place. The eyes express a triangular pattern from eye to eye and down to the mouth or chin. Eyes will wander briefly to other parts of the face, but majority of time will be looking at the eyes and lips. Gaze duration lasts in sections of four to five seconds then eyes move to the rest of the body, examining clothing, overall build, and jewellery. Both sexes, despite appropriate social norms, will glance over intimate areas of the body such as the crotch and breasts. Men tend to glance at women from the ground up, starting from the legs, then to the crotch, torso, breasts, shoulders, and then face. Some women find being scanned offensive, however, studies have shown that women too habitually scan men, they simply do it more discretely.

Double Wink

A single wink in western society can imply 'well done' (a good job), however, in contrast it can present as cheekiness, or between couples a low key sexual invitation. When done to someone new this can be offensive, therefore to avoid coming off too strong, the double wink, a wink done by blinking both eyes at the same time and holding them closed for a short time, along with a smile when eyes reopen can have a better affect.

Looking Up Through the Forehead

This is done by tilting the head at a forty-five degree angle, then looking upwards and is an expression that reflects childhood, because children look up to seek approval or permission. This is a submissive posture and due to the childlike nature, it evokes protective feelings, can gain sympathy from others and invokes another to assist. For example, when asking for directions a head tilt indicates no threat and shows that help is needed. Subconsciously, others see this as sincerity therefore they are more willing to be of support or service.

Head tilting with a smile can express meanings as well. A slow onset smile, a smile that gradually forms rather than a quick smile, indicates trustworthiness, not false, less dominant and can be more flirtatious Tilting the head is often perceived as more trustworthy rather than an upright head therefore it can be helpful in creating cooperative and favourable impressions, empathy and warmth, with just about everyone; and coupled with an honest slow smile can positively influence people.

Shifty and Darting Eyes

People assume that lying presents as shifty or darting eyes, however, as a predictor of a lie this is not the case. Looking away from a face helps us concentrate and eyes can wander for a variety of reasons rather than signalling mistrust such as; stress and nervousness or when put on the spot will cause the eyes to exhibit patterns that seem dishonest. However, research has shown that pathological liars are skilled in maintaining eye contact, more so then those who are honest. Liars track reactions and success of their lies, for this reason watching the face of another aids them in determining effectiveness or whether an adjustment is required. Therefore, when another is lying there is an increase rather than decrease in eye contact, and shifty eyes can present.

Darting eyes indicate that someone desires to exit from an undesirable circumstance. Eyes moving about a room can be to seek more stimulating interactions. Our eyes go to where our mind already is, and where our body wants to be. Eye patterns, need to observe carefully to determine the intent. Too much eye contact can be rude and unnatural, yet it is the unnatural that can signal the lie.

Eye Rolling

Eye rolling indicates disbelief such as; I can't believe you just said that. However, this non-verbal cue can be expressed in combination with the head tilting slightly to the side then stops before directly facing another, the eyes take over roll up and a scowl (dirty look) is formed. This indicates disapproval, distrust and suspicion.

The Eyebrows

Eyebrows are often very active in conversation and are an alternative to eye squinting. They crease to indicate anger or turn inward and down for disgust, raise to express surprise or a singular raise with one lower to indicate suspicion. When one eyebrow is raised and the other stays in its natural place, this expresses scepticism or displeasure. Yet when this is done subtly, with a slightly tilted head and a cheeky smile it indicates that someone finds something interesting.

Size, shape and placement of eyebrows portray meaning. Lower eyebrows present as more dominant whereas high eyebrows indicate submissiveness and a constant look of surprise. Eyebrows turned in to the outside of the face make the face appear concerned or empathetic. Bushy eyebrows signal dominance, and thin brows passiveness, whereas the mono-brow, where a single brow stretches across both eyes, presents as primitive, unsophisticated and un-groomed.

Eyebrows also have their own language; The eyebrow raise, where eyebrows go up and then down in one motion, express in speech to emphasis certain words, to pause and punctuate a point, or when answering questions.

When eyebrows raise and pause for a second this indicates a request for approval when unsure how others feel, or to verify if the message was understood. The pause waits for a gesture of approval such as a head nod or verbal agreement before lowering the brow. When there is no approval, then an eyebrow shrug expresses much like shrugging of the shoulders, indicating a lack of knowledge or even helplessness. However, when the raise, and pause is done with a slow raise of the head, this indicates disapproval. Disapproval is stronger if the head is lowered with the lips pursed tightly. This signals a desire to end communication altogether.

When someone wants to impress, flirt, or act animated the eyebrows move about continuously throughout a conversation and raised or arched eyebrows show positive feelings and high confidence.

Eye Avoidance Can Be Good

Studies have found that people who avoid eye contact while considering a response to a question have a seventy-two percent chance of answering correctly. When looking at faces, which are complex and a wealth of information we require a lot of mental processing and this disrupts thinking, therefore to provide a correct answer, gaze away and avoid eye contact.

Eye avoidance also controls hierarchy. Averting the eyes altogether, looking down and away with brief glances in the direction of someone who is aggressive can eliminate an attack response. This benefits both parties because it eliminates the chances of serious injury and the aggressor is satisfied because the signal indicates they are higher in the rank therefore, they feel they have won, will stop and turn away. Bullies always pick easy fights to build dominance, they do this because their insecure nature does not really to want to fight, they just want to rank higher.

Eye contact between humans and animals should also be considered. For example, eye contact with dogs or bears tends to bring about an attack as these animals perceive this as an aggressor, because with most animal species a stare is used to display dominance and aggression between members of the same species.

Looking away and avoiding eye contact indicates submissiveness and the least dominant is the first to look away. Test this out. Stare directly into their eyes of another for an extended period of time. Whoever breaks first will show lower rank. Direct and piercing eye contact lasts no longer than five seconds and will create a desire to look away. If staring is difficult, look at the area just above the eyes. Staring provokes stress, they will feel prey-like and under attack. Don't blink or narrow your eyes as this makes the dominance signal even more powerful.

Eye Trick to Predict

Eye movements are well known in neuro-linguistic programming (NLP), a system developed to aid in activating behavioural change and to improve communication. NLP aims at identifying the roots by which thoughts affect image, sound or feelings as well as understanding how others perceive particular circumstances. It focuses on change from unwanted results in reproducing the behaviour expressed in successful people so that others too, can be successful.

"Neuro" refers to the five senses; hearing, touch, smell, sight, taste. "Linguistic" refers to use of language, order of thought and behaviour. "Programming" echoes ideas and thought and organises them into actions.

The brain processes different information in different hemispheres. Tests have shown that eye movement is related to the part of the brain where we access thought and emotion. It also controls our motoring skills such as; right handed people tend to shift their heads and eyes to the right (left hemisphere) when processing logical and verbal tasks; and left handed people have the opposite patterns. The brain is cross-wired. The left hemisphere controls the right hand side of the body and right hemisphere controls the left. This is why we say left-handers are in their right minds!

A left-handed person has opposite meanings for eye-directions than that of the right-handed. Therefore, depending on the dominant hand people tend to look to the opposite side of the brain for answer.

Eye movement is also shown to be related to how people process information. When asked to do tasks that involved memory using sight, hearing or feeling; upward eye movements reflect visual processing, lateral (sideways) eye movements reflect auditory, processing and downward movements reflected either kinaesthetic (touch) or an inner thought or feeling.

Applying a psychic NLP eye trick;

Examine where people look as they attempt to recollect or express their thoughts.
- Right-handed people; eye movement up and to the left signals, accessing a visual memory.
- Movement up and right means, trying to construct a visual image.
- Eyes either right or left, but still level, indicate an auditory process such as remembering sounds and words.
- Eyes down and left indicate internal dialogue or self-talk.
- Down and right indicate a physical or habitual feeling.
- Straight ahead, unfocused or dilated, signals that visual or sensory information is being accessed.

Eye patterns are consistent for all right handed people except for very few exceptions. Left handed people tend to reverse from left to right and access information opposite to right handed people. Therefore, they tend to look down and left to access feelings instead of up and left.

These patterns can provide information that have predictive powers. By observing eye direction of others, we can interpret how they access information and how they internalise thought. This can be helpful when determining their intentions. Lying for example, right and up (constructed visual) and right and level (constructed auditory) both show that a person is trying to create or imagine new details about something whereas left and up (visual remembered) and left and level (auditory remembered) indicate that a person is remembering something that had actually happened.

Some people have habitual eye movements that have developed over time, these are the few exceptions, therefore someone who is highly visual may look up and left, or right, regardless of the type of question being asked. Someone who are touch (kinaesthetic) oriented may look down and right all the time even in reference to a thought about music or sound. However, even these cues give indication of the mindset and the type of person they are.

Here is a list of questions to determine type of learner/mindset you are communicating with so that you may tailor information to suit:
- Visual Remembered: Think of the colour of your first bike. Think of the first person you saw as you entered a room this morning.
- Visual Construction: Imagine what it would be like to fly. Imagine your dream car and pretend you are walking towards it, what do you see?

- Auditory Remembered: What was one of your favourite things someone said to you? What sounds do you enjoy the most?
- Auditory Constructed: What would a turtle sound like it if could talk? What would your parent say if they knew you were stealing money?
- Auditory Digital (Inner Self Talk): What sound does your inner voice make? What kind of inner discussion happens when you think of your children? When do you talk to yourself the most?
- Kinaesthetic Remembered (Tactile and Emotional): Imagine what sandpaper feels like against your skin. Imagine what a cat feels like when you pat it. Think of a time in your life when you felt proud for accomplishing something. When was the last time you were completely exhausted?
- Kinaesthetic Construction (Tactile and Emotional): Imagine the feeling of flour between your fingers that little by little becomes sticky instead of soft. Imagine the feeling of being helpless turns into powerful.

Mouth

Mouth expressions and movements can also reveal information in body language. For example, chewing on the bottom lip indicates feelings of worry, fear, or insecurity. Covering the mouth may be polite effort when yawning or coughing, yet it can also be an attempt to cover up a frown of disapproval. Smiling is one of the greatest body language signals, however, smiles can also be interpreted in many ways. A smile may be genuine, or it may be used to express false happiness, sarcasm, or even cynicism.

Here are examples of mouth, smile and lip signals:

Pursed lips: Tightening the lips indicates distaste, disapproval, or distrust.

Lip biting: Indicates a person is worried, anxious, or stressed.

Covering the mouth: When someone wants to hide an emotional reaction, they cover their mouth in order to avoid displaying smiles or smirks.

Turned up or down: Slight changes in the mouth are subtle indicators of what a person is feeling. The mouth is slightly turned up, indicates feeling happy or optimistic, slightly downturned mouth indicates sadness, disapproval, or even an outright sarcastic grimace.

Tight lipped with low intensity. The lips stretch across the face with no teeth showing. This smile has very little upward curl in the corner of the mouth and indicates a hidden attitude, thought, uncertainty, hesitation or lack of confidence. This smile is often used to pose for photographs when we are not in the mood, therefore it signals as a dishonest smile. It appears out of nervousness or stress, it can also appear when meeting new people.

Tight lipped with high intensity. This is a variation of the above smile with corners of the lips rising further with some teeth showing. The lips are slightly separated, the corners of the mouth are upturned, gaze is steady and warm; and the posture is relaxed. This smile appears when meeting new people, therefore it is not entirely a full honest smile, however, it does show openness to others.

Uneven smile. This is where only one side of the face stretches to smile and the other side does not. The opposite side may even be down turned or frowning. This smile depicts frame of mind such as; cheeky humour, and sarcasm.

Upper smile. The upper lid is raised to expose only the top row of teeth, and the lower teeth remain hidden. The jaw and lower teeth remain closed and expresses as insecure or with a hidden agenda.

Grin or smirk. This indicates smugness and arrogance. It is a tight lipped smile with a degree of self-satisfaction. A nervous smile often appears like a smirk, but they are not to be confused. The smirk expresses dominant body language such as head back, shoulders back, open postures along with verbal pride. Sometimes though the smirk is due to stress of being confronted.

Broad smile. The upper and lower teeth are made visible. The gaze is relaxed and the expresses as joy and pleasure. This is a true smile and not one that is easily faked. A signal of an honest smile is the appearance of crow's feet to the corners of the eyes. Crow's feet make it seem as though the eyes are smiling, and it is difficult to replicate this smile without being truly happy because the muscles are usually out of our conscious control.

Reverse smile. The mouth is inverted into a down-facing u shape and indicates high stress, unhappiness, anger, tension and depression.

Laughter

Laughter IS the best medicine and studies have shown that laughter can help protect the health of the heart, increase tolerance to pain, boost the immune system by producing antibodies, reduce blood pressure and overall anxiety, it can even extend life. Whether a laugh is natural, or forced, the body does not know the difference.

Habitual angry and hostile people result in more heart attacks and those who are depressed have higher chances of heart disease. Every part of our bodies benefits from laughter, laughter reduces stress, and stress is the biggest culprit for creating dis-ease in the body.

When we laugh, stress related hormones decrease significantly. Chronically ill patients show immediate symptom relief with laughter, the need for sedative is reduced, and overall pain decreases. Laughter also increases immune function and healing. Therefore, laugh often.

Honest Smile and Shrugs

Smiles are controlled by two muscles, the consciously controlled zygomatic major muscles, these run down the side of the face and connect to corners of the mouth, and the ones used when we smile for the camera. The other orbicularis oculi muscles are unconsciously expressed and pull eyes back. Orbicularis muscles are important in body language as they are the producers of smiling eyes (crow's feet), where wrinkling shows at the corner of eyes. This is an indication of genuine automatic happiness. Therefore, appearance of crow's feet is an indicator for determining genuine enjoyment. Another indicator is the corner of eyes turn downwards and the eyebrows will dip as well. A natural, genuine smile has symmetry where the face is even on both sides because the brain responds to pleasure.

Insincere smiles appear as exposed teeth and stretched lips across the face with no wrinkles in the eyes. Crow's feet cannot be faked because this ends up looking like a squished face and the genuine smile is innate, not taught, even people born blind smile to display happiness. Fake smiles are more pronounced on the left side of the face since they are consciously being controlled much like an uneven shoulder shrugs which indicates dishonesty and not knowing something. When truthful, shoulders will come up in unison and sharply, however, if just one shoulder comes up and only slightly this indicates uncertainty with what one has stated.

Dishonesty expresses through body language to support an emotion, if the emotion lacks harmony, the body lacks symmetry. Shoulder shrugs are gravity defying body language cues, meaning it requires energy and commitment, without this it only meets half way. When weak smiles or shoulders only partially come this indicates that someone is misleading about their true thoughts and feelings.

Liars also have difficulty smiling, however if they do, it presents as a forced and strained expression with underlying stress. Smiling is a subconsciously submissive gesture and liars often worry about being caught and feel that smiling might give them away, instead they try to appear expressionless. Smiling can therefore be an effective way to display honesty, although smiling too large, for too long or at inappropriate times will have the reverse effect.

Smiling, even if fake, can be effective in influencing other's thoughts, emotions and opinions. If you smile, and frequently, it can rub off on those around you. This can be very beneficial to others especially to ourselves because we can trick the mind to an intended emotion.

Facial expressions are geared to help those that hold them rather than those who view them. As stated in an earlier chapter experiments have shown that by forcing a fake smile we can trick our brain into happiness. Our facial expression reflects our inner emotions; however, this same linkage works both ways. Expressions we make are a reflection of our moods, however, we can change a mood, and this can influence our expression, therefore we should change a facial expression, not because we feel happier, but because it will help us to feel happy. Our minds are emotionally hardwired to mirror expressions that show up on our face, when we change our facial expression, the brain begins to mirror this and flows into a process of creating currents to amplify this state.

Chapter 9
Faking and Micro Expressions

Body language cues is a skill that can be learned, just as you are learning by reading this book, therefore, with knowledge it can be faked such as; keeping hands out of pockets, using hands in ways to express honesty and openness, or keeping the hands away from the face to signal confidence, and this becomes easier through conscious thought and repetition. However, there are other cues that are more difficult to control.

Micro expressions are signals that can separate liars from truth tellers. Micro expressions appear as furrows, smirks, frowns, smiles and wrinkles and they express accurate truth of the emotions. However, they are called micro because these completely honest gestures present suddenly, momentarily and vanish fast. They are controlled by muscles and are provoked by underlying emotions that are almost impossible to control with conscious effort. An example is the fake smile. Though this is obvious because lips are pulled across the mouth, the muscles controlling the eyes, are not participating.

If you were to record someone then upon playback slow the video down, it would be easier to detect the expressions. Micro expressions may be difficult to detect and control however, the rest of the body language will indicate that they exist, and just because these happen so fast, it does not mean they cannot be identified.

Our subconscious intuition is always giving us a sixth sense feeling. When we feel mistrust with another, yet, we have no explanation for it, a combination of micro expressions and our intuition is at play. While our faces are largely under our control, we are unable to diligently be attentive to it, because other body parts, including our verbal communication requires our attention as well. . When we talk, see, or do, our faces naturally respond to what is going on around us because they are closely tied to our mind and our emotions. We have a cause and effect relationship with our mind, the face provides distractions with a vast amount of information that we tune into, hence there is too much for purely one focus.

A way of noticing faking is to observe conflicting body language. Inconsistencies where the words being spoken, do not match the non-verbal language.

Breathing

Mirroring a person's breathing pattern can create a mutual understanding and the pattern of breathing can indicate someone's mood and state of mind. Deeper breathing uses the diaphragm and abdomen, this indicates a relaxed and confident signal. Shallow, and rapid breathing indicates a more nervous or anxious signal. When someone is faking a smile, the body does not participate in disguising the breath. The body expresses discomfort by increasing the heart rate along with breath rate, this then can create; sweating, a change in normal colour to the face or neck, trembling or shaking of hands/lips, or fidgeting.

Chapter 10
Posture and Personal Space

Posture

The term posture refers to how we hold our bodies as well as the overall physical form of an individual. Posture can convey a wealth of information about how a person is feeling it also gives hints about personality characteristics, such as whether a person is confident, open, or submissive. For example; sitting up straight indicates that a person is focused and paying attention to what's going on. The body hunched forward indicates boredom or indifference.

When observing body language, watch for signals from the posture;

Open posture - the torso is open and exposed, this indicates friendliness, openness, and willingness.

Closed posture – the torso often hunches forward, the arms and legs crossed, this indicates hostility, unfriendliness, and anxiety.

Personal Space

Many have said, 'I need my personal space'. When someone is a little to close, and within our personal field. This can make us feel uncomfortable.

Proxemics refers to the distance between people as they interact. Just as body movements and facial expressions can communicate a great deal of non-verbal information, so can this physical space between individuals.

There are four guidelines for social distance that occur in different situations:

Intimate distance— 6 to 18 inches: This level of physical distance often indicates a closer relationship or greater comfort between individuals. It usually occurs during intimate contact such as hugging, whispering, or touching.

Personal distance— 1.5 to 4 feet: Physical distance at this level usually occurs between people who are family members or close friends. The closer the people can comfortably stand while interacting can be an indicator of the level of intimacy in their relationship.

Social distance— 4 to 12 feet: This level of physical distance is often used with individuals who are acquaintances. With a co-worker you see several times a week and know very well, you may feel more comfortable interacting at a closer distance. However, when you do not know the other person well, such as a sales assistant you only see once a month, a distance of 10 to 12 feet may feel more comfortable.

Public distance— 12 to 25 feet: Physical distance at this level is often used in public speaking situations. Presenting in front of students or at work are examples of this situation.

It is also important to note that the level of personal distance that individuals require for comfort can vary from culture to culture. An example is the difference between people from European cultures and those from North America. People from Italy tend to feel more comfortable standing closer to one another as they interact while those from North America need more personal distance.

Gestures

Waving, pointing, and using fingers to indicate numerical amounts are common and easy to understand gestures. Some gestures may be cultural, however, giving a thumbs-up or a peace sign in another country might have a completely different meaning than it does in Australia.

The following examples are just a few common gestures and their possible meanings:

A clenched fist can indicate anger in some situations or solidarity in others.

A thumb up and thumbs down are often used as gestures of approval and disapproval.

The 'okay' gesture, touching the thumb to the index finger in a circle with remaining fingers pointing upward can mean okay or all right. However, in some parts of Europe, the same signal is used to imply you are nothing and is viewed as an insult, and in some South American countries, the symbol is considered to be a vulgar gesture.

The V sign, the index and middle finger point upwards and separate to form a V-shape. This means peace or victory in some countries. In Australia, the symbol takes on an offensive meaning when the back of the hand is facing outward.

Arms and Legs

Crossing arms can indicate defensiveness. Crossing legs away from another person may indicate dislike or discomfort with that individual. Other subtle signals such as expanding arms widely can be an attempt to seem larger or more commanding, while keeping arms close to the body can be an effort to minimize oneself or withdraw from attention.

When evaluating body language, observe signals that arms, and legs convey:

Crossed arms indicate defensiveness, self-protection, or closed-off.

Standing with hands placed on the hips indicates someone is ready and in control, or a sign of aggressiveness.

Clasping the hands behind the back indicates feeling bored, anxious, or even angry.

Rapidly tapping fingers or fidgeting indicates boredom, impatience, or frustration.

Crossed legs indicates being closed off or in need of privacy.

Chapter 11
Reading the Signs

This chapter contains examples of common body language expressions from various categories. The last chapter in this book you will find an A to Z dictionary for more gesture and signal indications.

Signals indicating interest

It is important to know if people are interested in what you are saying; otherwise, you are just wasting your time. Imagine you are a Geography teacher. You have always been interested in Geography, so you assume that your students feel the same way as you do. But are they really interested? Are your teaching methods good enough to arouse their interest? Unless you can recognize the different body signals your students are conveying, you would never know how they are adapting to the subject matter. And unless you find out if staring continuously at you without blinking the eyes is a sign of interest or an indication of being in dreamland, you could not take the necessary steps to adjust to their learning needs.

Here are some signals expressed by people who are interested in what you are saying:

- They maintain eye contact more than 60% of the time. The more wide opened eyes are, the more interest there is. A person maintains eye contact more when listening than when talking. Heads are inclined forward. They are nodding their heads indicating attentiveness, listening, and they agree with you. Feet are pointing towards you. They smile frequently, however, not all smiles convey the same feeling. An oblong smile is not genuine. Where lips are withheld completely back from the upper and lower teeth, forming the oblong shape. This is used to show courtesy, not happiness or friendliness, also expressed when enjoying a lame joke.

Signals indicating that a person is Open to agree with you

When you were a young child, did you attempt to decode the facial expressions of your parents when you ask them to buy you a new toy or to take you to Disneyland? A frown would likely be a "No!" yet a nod would make you jump with joy. As you grow older, it has become a necessity to detect if another agrees with your decision or proposal. This is an ability that aids negotiators, employees, and even lovers to succeed in their ventures because they would be able to change their approach early enough to adjust to a specific situation. There are signals to indicate if people are more receptive to accepting your ideas:

Hands are flat on the table. Palms are open genuineness. Stroking the chin indicates they are thinking and may agree with you after careful evaluation. Heads are inclined forward. Nodding their heads. Legs are spaced out from each other. They smile frequently. They unbutton jackets indicating friendliness and willingness to collaborate with you. Hands on the chest. This signifies openness and conveys sincerity, honesty, or dedication. However, a woman putting her hands in her breast is a defensive position and may indicate that she is surprised or astonished.

How to know if a person is thinking

People think all the time, however, individuals express different body movements based on the type and intensity of their thinking. Some of their actions are:

Stroking the chin, they are assessing the advantages and disadvantages of the proposal/idea being presented. They take their glasses off, after which they may either clean them, or put the tip of the frame in their mouth. This indicates buying some time to think things over. A frame in the mouth also indicates a need for more details and they are willing to listen. They are pinching the bridge of the nose often with eyes closed. Someone is engaged in very deep thought when doing this.

They may be involved in a difficult situation, where they are aware of the consequences that may occur as a result of making crucial decisions. Palm below the chin, index finger pointed and extended along the cheek, remaining fingers placed beneath the mouth. This gesture indicates thoughts that are criticizing. They walk with the head down and hands behind the back. This indicates someone is worried about their problems, and they are thinking of ways to solve them.

Signals indicating frustration or dismay

A coach whose team loses by a point may grunt "Aaarrrrrrr!" or be silent whilst expressing body movements that indicate disappointment.

Here are some indicators for frustration;

They scratch or rub the hair, or the back of the neck.

You often hear the word "Tsk." Or they kick the dust or air.

How action-oriented people Act or move

People who are goal-oriented and highly motivated are recognized by how they speak yet their actions speak louder.

They walk at a fast rate while swinging their arms loosely. Hands on their hips, usually with legs apart. They walk with hands on their hips indicating a spurt of vitality in the moment, which can be followed by sluggishness.

How to know if a person is keeping a secret Defensive/Hiding Something

The mouth might keep a secret, but gestures indicate that people are hiding something they do not want others to find out, such as: They walk with their hands in their pockets. Cross their arms. Hide their hands any way they can.

Signals indicating boredom

Imagine your boss is doing a presentation and all employees are required to listen. You noticed that many click their pen, tap their feet, and drum their fingers. After the meeting, you hear the boss ask them, "Did you enjoy the presentation?" They say "Definitely!" But you know better. Their actions indicated just how bored they were. Some signals conveyed by people who are bored and disinterested include:
Head supported by the palm, often accompanied by drooping eyes. They show inattentiveness by staring at a blank space (eyes not blinking) or by looking around frequently. Pulling their ears. This also indicates someone wanting to interrupt while another is talking. Clicking a pen non-stop. Tapping hands or feet. Yawn incessantly. Feet or other body parts are pointing to the exit, indicating they are very eager to leave. They move restlessly in their seats. This can also indicate lack of ease, or exhaustion. They cross legs and constantly kick their foot in a very slight motion.

When presenting if you notice signals of boredom, do not start talking faster or louder. Restrain from this even though instinct tells you to do so. Instead, ask them to comment on what and how you are speaking, and listen to what they have to say. You may discover what's actually preventing them from keeping up with you.

Signals conveying excitement

If you have experienced getting a promotion, receiving a special gift, or winning a contest, this can express excitement. Some movements include:
Rubbing palms against each other. Clapping hands. Heads tilt forward. Crossing fingers (hope that something big or special will happen).

Signals Exhibiting Confidence/Authority/Power

People with a high degree of self-confidence are more likely to be successful than those who have low self-esteem. Moreover, those who exhibit authority or dominance usually come out on top because they subconsciously make other people feel weaker. So how do they move?

- They maintain firm eye contact and rarely look at other body parts that are under the nose. They speak with a low-pitched, slow-paced, and downward-inflected voice. Chin tilted upwards. Chest projected outwards. They maintain an erect posture, whether standing or sitting. They sit in reverse, with the back of the chair serving as their support or shield. This indicates bossy and aggressive. Hands are clenched behind the back or beside the hips. Feet are on top of the table. Firm handshake, palms pointing downwards. They lean back with both hands supporting the head. They move with precision and with no hesitation. They walk solidly with forceful arm swings. Join the fingertips of both hands together (small finger of both hands joined together, ring finger of both hands joined together, and so on). Palms of both hands are not in contact with each other. The higher the hands are elevated, the more confident they are. Extend one leg over the arm of a chair, this indicates disinterest, or unconcerned. The, I don't care attitude.

You can express domination by rising or elevating yourself. Choose a chair or location where others have to "look up". Subconsciously this creates one to feel weaker and can easily be manipulated.

Body movements that signal Anger and resistance

Many rarely let their anger get out of control, they are more likely to restrain their raging emotions, however, sometimes people can snap. Recognising signals that express wrath or resistance can prevent chances of the fireworks exploding. Here are some indications:

Fists are clenched. Hands or feet are tapping. One hand is clutching the other hand, arm, or elbow. Arms are crossed over the chest. Eyes are blinking constantly. Pulling collar away from the neck, much like letting air in during a hot day in the summer. They kick the dust or air. Arms are on the table with hands gripping the edge. Observe context with this as it can mean "You better get this done or else!" or "Better listen or you'll regret this!"

Body movements that signal nervousness or tension

Signals conveyed by nervous people include:

Fists are clenched. Hands or feet are tapping. Bottom edges between the fingers of one hand are clenched with the bottom edges between the fingers of the other hand. Much like praying. Hands are interlocked (flesh between thumb and index finger of one hand joined with flesh between thumb and index finger of another hand) and pressing each other. Speak in a high-pitched, fast-paced, stuttering voice. Whistle to conceal and fight their nervousness. Often clearing the throat. One hand is clutching the other hand, wrist, arm, or elbow. Arms are at the back, with one hand pressing the wrist or arm. Arms are crossed, but they are gripping their biceps. Legs are crossed while standing. Weak handshake, palms pointing upwards. Eyes avoid contact. Ankles are locked or glued to each other. When accompanied by clenched fists, this indicates holding back strong emotions or feelings.

How to know if a person is doubting or Suspicious of you

Are you regarded as a trustworthy person, or thought of as someone who is full of nonsense? Here are some indicators for suspicion:

They glimpse sideways from the corner of one eye. Rubbing or touching eyes or ears. Hands are tucked in pockets. Arms are crossed over the chest. Eye glasses drop to the lower bridge of the nose, with eyes peering over them. This can also indicate being examined closely (to the point that you get conscious).

When someone is doubting themselves, they rub or touch the nose. This subconsciously presents when someone is uncertain of an answer to a critical question or when they are concerned of others reaction to their answer.

Signals when someone requires reassurance

Some people feel that they are always making the wrong decisions. "Should I really buy this? "Maybe I should ask." "Can I really get a better job?" These people do certain actions to reassure themselves that they have made the right choice, and that everything will be okay.

They stick a pen in their mouth. Squeeze the chunky part of their hand. Rub the back of the chair (while sitting). Clamp their hands with thumbs touching against one another. Bite their nails (in some cases). Touch the throat. Jiggle coins in their pockets. (For those who are concerned about their riches).

When someone is wanting to reassure others they:

- Hold both hands and sometimes hug. The facial expression matches the solemn mood of the other. Shake the others hand with their right hand and cup it with the left hand.

Indications of pride

People often show how proud they are of material possession such as a car by leaning against it or by touching it. They express a sparkle in their eyes and a thrill in their voice.

How to detect a liar

People lie for a variety of reasons. It may be to cover up a fault, embarrassment, to avoid upsetting others, to encourage when hope is lacking, or to be spared from petty hassles.

Here are some indications conveyed by people when lying:

They speak in a high-pitched, fast-paced, stuttering voice. They are constantly swallowing and clearing their throat. They try their best to avoid eye contact. This applies particularly to people who want to avoid discussing a certain topic otherwise they maintain long eye contact to watch if the facial expression of the receiver knows about the deception. They look somewhere else and glimpse from the corner of their eye. They stick the tongue out to moist their lips. Blink rapidly. Rub the throat. Arms are crossed over the chest.

- They are constantly touching parts of the face, especially the mouth, ear, and nose as if covering them. Scratch the head or back of the neck. Body language is closed, descending, and insecure. Hands or feet are tapping. Always looking down with shrugged shoulders. Constantly moving from one place to another or changing postures. Pointing parts of their body (feet) to an escape route (door).

Avoid jumping to conclusions

Although silence usually indicates someone is reserved and relaxed, some can hold anger within and stay quiet. A wide open mouth indicates shock or astonishment for one person, while another person who expresses this gesture could just be concentrating intently on a task. Constantly touching the mouth indicates lying, although the real reason may just be an itchy mouth.

Observe other signals being expressed before conclusion. Judgment based on one or two gestures may not be accurate enough, although they can be dependable. Observe context and combine these observations with the spoken words for more insights to inner feelings of another.

Chapter 12
Automatic Psychological States

Happy, sad or many other emotions can be obvious, however, what is behind some emotional states that seem beyond the obvious? Here are some automatic responses that are psychological conditions. These conditions conceal communication of true feelings and thoughts, yet, they too are body language signals:

Dysphoria- This is general state of sadness that includes restlessness, lack of energy, anxiety, and vague irritation. It is the opposite of euphoria and is different from typical sadness because it often includes a kind of jumpiness and some anger. This response can present due to a distressing situation, extreme boredom, or depression.

Normopathy- These are people who are so focused on blending in and conforming to social norms that it becomes a manic response. A person who is normotic is often fixated on having no personality at all, and only doing exactly what is expected by society. Many people experience mild normopathy at various times in their lives, especially when trying to fit into a new social situation, or when trying to conceal habits they believe others would reject. Body language reveals the discomfort in these situations.

Repetition compulsion - Freud's famous definition, "the desire to return to an earlier state of things." Repetition compulsion is something people experience quite often. This is the urge to do something again and again, for example; ordering the same thing at your favourite restaurant or driving home by the same route. Body language can present as anxiety if change is considered.

Group feelings- There are some feelings we have as members of a group or society. These are called intergroup feelings. Family members are also intergroup members. Feelings associated with groups are noticed when they are in contradiction with our personal feelings. Group feelings often cause painful contradictions. A person may have an intragroup feeling that homosexuality is morally wrong, yet, they may personally have homosexual feelings. Likewise, a person may have an intragroup feeling that certain races or religions are inferior, yet they personally know people from these races and religions whom they consider friends. A group feeling can only come about through collective suggestion and isn't something that we would ever have on our own. Body language reveals these contradictory beliefs.

Chapter 13
Subconscious Mirroring

Most people are oblivious to the messages and the impact they have on others and this is especially true with mirroring. Mirroring is the subconscious replication of nonverbal signals. It is instinctive, automatic and mostly without awareness. This occurs in everyday interactions, and often goes unnoticed by the receiver as well as the individual who is being mirrored. As two or more people interact they begin to display similar nonverbal gestures, this can make them believe that they share similar attitudes and ideas, however, it is the mirror neurons which react and cause these responses. This replication done by the neurons enable the individuals to feel a greater sense of engagement, bonding and understanding; and this can be a positive happy replication or the negative such as, 'I'm on your side', anger.

The discovery of the mirror neuron shows that a specific set of neurons respond to outer stimuli. When someone observes another these neurons respond as if the motion was actually performed, when in reality the movement was merely observed. Scans show that the area of the brain where these neurons reside light up when action is performed, and the same area lights up when someone is just watching others perform actions.

The mirror neuron stems from imitative learning and begins as early as infancy, because babies begin to mimic those around them to establish connections with particular body movements. This practice of mimicry aids the baby/infant in establishing a sense of empathy and this begins the process in understanding another's emotions. This mimicry continues as we grow, it strengthens with practice and we develop unconscious competency in relating to others by connecting to their emotions; and we do this by mirroring their movements, involuntarily and automatically.

Mirroring not only consists of gestures, we also unconsciously mimic speech patterns, and attitudes. An obvious reaction of mirroring is yawning or smiling. When another yawns or smiles, we are triggered to yawn or smile, even just an image or words can trigger the mirror neuron. For example, when we view pictures of people who display happiness, disgust, fear or pain, we react to them as if we had felt it ourselves.

This ability to connect with people, even strangers, has an important function in our daily lives since it allows us to build and hold relationships, creates sympathy, and inhibit fighting. Emotions have inward and outward forces with varying strengths. With some practice we can either resist outward stimuli or use it to transmute inward stimuli. In other words, the mind will follow and become the inner feeling and outer expression. For example: Uncrossing the arms or unfurrowing the brow can present as open and happy gesture, yet simply doing this can make us feel happy, as does smiling, even if one is not in the mood, a forced smile can transmute the mind in feeling better and therefore it can set the framework by which an interaction takes place as well.

Though mirroring occurs unconsciously, and we adopt the gestures of another, mirroring can also be done intentionally, and the mind will do the same. The mirror neuron triggers the subconscious mind in recognizing the pattern of faces and facial expressions such as smiling or frowning faces; and responds accordingly by copying then relaying the motion and becomes the emotionally felt outer pattern. An intentional practice in mirroring has the same affect, however, it is important to understand that mirroring is distinct from intentional mirroring, as this is calculated imitation to copy another in order to achieve a desired outcome.

When intentionally mirroring we should act with courtesy and caution. Never let another be aware of what we are doing as this can be viewed as copying and mocking them, such as; they stand, you stand. They scratch the head, you scratch your head. This expresses insult and can irate another.

The main objective for intentional mirroring is to influence ease by duplicating another's mannerism, this places you both on the same level. It is non-verbal way to say 'I am like you, I feel the same'. This synchronicity gives a secure feeling and ease, 'the vibes are right'. This is because the same emotions are experienced therefore mutual trust, connection and understanding emerges. Synchronicity can also be created through music for example; when playing background music during a romantic date the frequency of the sound links the two on the same wave-length.

Corresponding with moods

When someone is association with others that have accents such as; a group of friends or during overseas travel, they will begin to mirror the verbal accent. The mind responds to where the physical exposure is and adopts accents or mannerisms to fit in better. Studies have shown that the more we imitate others, the more we begin to be like them and in turn, they become like us. Mirroring can be a helpful characteristic with our non-verbal communication as it shows others that we like them and are connecting with them.

It is difficult for many to remain expressionless when another is facing them with a happy or angry expression. It's even more difficult to smile at sad faces or make sad faces at laughing faces. The unconscious mind exerts more control over our faces then we think. While it is somewhat possible to control our reactions, a great deal of mental power is required to reverse our natural inherent tendencies. This is why an honest smile is unable to express to at a sad face, if someone tries, subtle spontaneous twitches reveal true responses, and these responses indicate that we actually feel sad for the other. This example gives meaning to the statement, 'we are all connected'.

We should be very careful about our facial expressions and gestures since they will necessarily have a profound effect on others. Our expressions and body gestures illicit similar responses from others, so if we want to make people happy, we should smile more and use more expressive body language. In turn, others around us will naturally mimic our gestures.

When someone has concerns do not express a joyous signal and say, "Don't worry about it. Let's do something so you can forget about what's bugging you." This person is in a low mood. Their subconscious expects empathy. Match the disposition first, say something like, "I feel sad for you. If there's anything I can do to help, just let me know." Often, people just want another to be in the same mood as they are, happy, sad, angry and so on.

Be mindful though, when we intentionally mirror emotional problems of others, we risk absorbing their emotions. Therefore, avoiding heightened negative emotions would be good practice. However, imitation of a smile, and holding it for a period of time, will create happiness, and gestures that display confidence, will actually make you feel confident, regardless of how you feel initially. When seated during a conversation, connect your fingertips of one hand to the other and press them against each other, much like a triangle (do not press the palms together). Do this, and you will trigger the subconscious into believing you are feeling confident.

Intentional Mirroring Practices

Often, we are not adept at understanding why we feel the way we do. More often than not, we just feel the sensations that our subconscious relays and our bodies ignorantly give alibi to them through our body language. Others in our interactions are also in the dark when it comes to knowing why they feel the way they do, just as most when asked the question, what do you want in life often reply vaguely and non-specifically, 'to be happy'. But what does happiness mean to them! When others express unknown emotions, we can use mirroring to uplift their mood, we can even use it to increase attraction and rapport.

Who would you rather be with, a grump, a happy person, an anxious person or someone who is relaxed?

The answer is simple. You would want to be around people who have the same behaviors, attitudes, and values as yours, including those that you trust.

To build trust with another we must exhibit the same qualities as that person. We can do this by;

Mirroring them, matching their facial expression, gestures, posture, speech, style, actions, breathing patterns, values and beliefs. When we do this, we also match their way of thinking which aids in observing inner thoughts and views. When we are aware of a desire outcome, we are able to control and direct a conversation… and even affect how people feel about us. Here are some examples to create a magnetic connection.

Assume They Already Like You

Get out of your own way! We treat new connections as though it were a challenge, and some can only be approved by passing several personality checks. When meeting new people, we are often wary because there is an array of impressions that we have through our conditioned beliefs such as; I hope they are nice, do they like me, are they freeloaders, what do they really want and so on. This is quite ironic, because if you feel this and I feel this, then it's quite likely many others feel the same, after all we do have similar, inherent subconscious patterning.

Many people are willing to give others a chance, especially when the right of signals are expressed. When you assume that you are *already* friends, the subconscious mind will relax. We are naturally feel comfortable when we are with others that like us, our body language is more open, and our speech is warmer and friendlier. People instinctively respond to warmth. Therefore, believe that they like you and they *will* like you. It's a win/win for both of you.

Me, in conversation

An important part of connection is feeling like the other understands you on a meaningful level and are on your wavelength. You can do this by emphasising similarities such as; places of interest, foods, or activities. However, we must be mindful of the 'me 'in our verbal communication. Give others a chance to share information about themselves, because the mind responds as if this was mutual conversation and begins to believe the information is about another. In other words, the more one speaks of themselves the more they like the listener and feel similarities, when in fact they are really liking themselves. They also assume it to be a great conversation even if the other does not speak much.

Verbal communication is a part of interaction, however, it not as impactful as body language when expressing "we are the same". When another is speaking our gestures do most of the work. Therefore, a subtle way of connecting is by mirroring another.

Pace and Lead

When another is feeling low, rather than matching their gestures we can take the lead. Just as skilled conversationalists can direct where a conversation goes, we can prompt another to mirror us. This is known as pacing and leading, here is how:

At first match another's gestures to establish rapport and ease. When you see that they are in a more open posture start with a small change in your gesture. Cross (or uncross) your legs, tilt your head, change the tone of your voice and watch how they respond; if they match your change, then you know that you're in sync. At this point, you are in a position to present more small changes that can completely alter the tone of the interaction. For example, by mirroring someone who is upset, you can slowly present calmer and more open body language. Or, to build excitement express excited behaviour such as a higher voice pitch, and comical hand gestures.

Synchronicity and Remote Mirroring

The ultimate goal of mirroring is to build rapport (harmony). Mirroring is the time when you and others feel close and in synchronicity with each other, and it can feel like you have known each other for years.

So how would you know if rapport has been built?

Mirror them. Match whatever characteristic, or behavior they express that you would like to reflect.

After some time of doing this, touch your nose or cross your legs. If they do the same thing, you have received a signal that indicates harmony. This has lowered defense, created open body language and they are more receptive to your suggestions.

Rapport can even be built by mirroring from a distant, known as remote mirroring:

- Relax, clear your mind of all negative thoughts and create a bond by focusing on the entire body of someone you wish to mirror. Make their image real and vivid, with colour, scent, and if you can, hear their breath.
- Think of what they may be doing at the moment, then replicate the actions, and behaviors.
- Use your subconscious to enter their world. Feel them, feel the connection. Emit positive sensations and feel them uniting their entire person into yours.

With this exercise, you can even mirror those you admire (role models), help another with relief or intend warmth and joy. Try remote mirroring and you will soon see some astounding results. This just as body english can be likened to remote intention setting. (Refer to Chapter 4; the Basics in Body Language for a refresher). It reveals the potential we have to make real change with our thoughts. Remote mirroring, remote intention, conscious intent and body English teaches us, Michael Jordon, the bowlers, ice hockey players, Lynne McTaggart, the healers, even Einstein that we are connected to everyone and everything. And that we all are capable of expansive possibilities. After all, we are the alchemists.

Mirroring and Smiling

Research has shown that our facial muscles subconsciously mirror what we see in others. While it is possible to control our facial muscles by consciously over-ridding this tendency, most by nature, will imitate what they see in others. This is why it is important to, both imitate smiles when seen, and to avoid expressing a bitter face.

Smiling is contagious and often just by holding a smile others feel compelled to smile as well. This same process occurs with attitudes of those surrounding us. Persistent negative attitudes from others around us can deflate our energy and drag down our moods. Whereas, optimistic attitudes make us feel better. Here is an example:

After a long day at work the husband comes home with a scowl on his face and drops himself upon the couch. He's had a bad day, and so too has the wife. Their expressions feed one another, and their attitudes remains negative. What if... the husband came home with a smile due to good news? Regardless of her day, if the husband takes the lead and persists with his expression, his wife will follow, and both are happy. If one or the other fails to follow the lead, the entire mood would be soured by the frowning party. Both parties are therefore responsible for deciding the mood.

Often, we are distracted with daily habits and customs, that when we are around someone in a bad mood, when do not consider (or unaware of) the importance in initiating a smile, even a fake smile when held persistently will transmute the circumstance.

Try this experiment; see just how difficult it is to frown when viewing smiles or smile when viewing frowning.

Smiling at a random stranger can flood their body with positive hormones and brighten their day. Even just holding a smile despite feeling down can help elevate your mood and make you feel better.

Chapter 14
Body Language in Negotiations

In almost every point in our life, we unconsciously do the art of negotiations. From haggling at a market stall, persuading for a well-deserved income increase, to getting a child to eat vegetables for a reward. Negotiations are being made daily in our life, and almost all aspects of the negotiation process involve body language. For example; thumbs up, open hands, a closed fist, or closed body language. In business negotiations, expression of body language is important for outcome. Reading body movements of your counterparts and making the right gestures may spell the difference between success and failure in the negotiation process.

Body language begins the moment you walk into the negotiation area, before person to person contact. Be keen by observing the whole body language of whoever/s is present during the negotiation particularly - the head, arms, hands, chest, stomach, legs and feet.

Power of First Impression

When negotiating, the first move is the most crucial. Just like in a game of chess, if you play the white piece, you have the first move, and the opponent's next move is dependent on your first move. Therefore, a firm and calculated move with positive body language will work in your favour. Project a solid handshake by holding the hand firmly, do not squeeze it. Tighten the grip slightly, one time while looking at the eyes. Pressing the hand once or twice indicates excitement or vitality, more than this can make another uneasy. Radiate your enthusiasm by looking at the eyes with sincerity. If you cannot maintain eye contact, it can be viewed as hiding something or lack of sincerity.

Use your Body Language Knowledge

During the negotiation observe gestures, notice if there is interest in what you are saying, if they are casting doubts, are they open to accept your proposal, and even when they are lying. Be alert in recognizing these signals, moreover, be aware of your own expressions. You may be exhibiting signals of nervousness without awareness, and your counterparts (who may also know body language) can take advantage of the circumstances.

Personal Space Negotiation

At the negotiating table, even while standing, each person creates their own personal space, their own territory. People of higher status such as president of a company, command more personal space, and are often accompanied by advisors. The most dominant chair, often one at the far end of a table is the most dominant (the head of the table) and the symbol of authority and power. If another occupies the dominant chair, a good negotiator can alter this by strategic seating arrangements by placing allies in such a way to surround a dominator, or any seating arrangement where they are at a comfortable advantage.

Chapter 15
Body Language in Selling

Studies in Psychology tell us the effect we have on others depends on seven percent of what we say from the mouth, thirty eight percent being the manner in which we say it (how we sound), and fifty five percent by our body language. Though words can be effective in communication, it is the ninety three percent of body language and manner (sound) which conveys emotion, and this can be expressed without saying the actual words.

Emotions are automatically expressed when selling. In the physical world, we sell tangible items and ideas, and a concise as well as effective way to sell is through body language. When selling, we can use postures, facial expressions, gestures, mannerisms, and our physical appearance to close the sale successfully. Most customers tend to buy when triggered by their senses. The key here is to do everything you can to positively affect the senses.

Non-verbal communication denotes that a man of few words is a man of credibility. It is often not what you say that influences others; it is what you do not say, the gestures that express comprehension, disposition, morality, and compassion are the influencers. The moment of meeting a potential buyer is the instant where you are being assessed based on your influencers along with image, and this perception is decided in a span of ten seconds or less. This is a crucial moment in selling, as first impression will leave a permanent mark. Whether you make or break a sale can depend purely on the non-verbal signals you express during first contact.

In establishing how well or not first impression is viewed, observe the signals from the potential buyer, however, be mindful of assumption. For example, shaking legs might indicate that a person is nervous, there may be lack in trust, yet, it may just be a person's natural behavior. A person's eyes may evade you because they are hiding something, or it could indicate being shy.

Here are some body language techniques to assist in sales:
- You can immediately analyse personality by studying style in handshakes. An assertive person holds your hand firmly, someone with little or no confidence often gives a frail handshake. A person who wants to win your trust shakes

your hand with the other hand covering the shake or holding your elbow. Adopt a handshake that is firm, yet not crushing. Convey confidence and professionalism, not dominance.

- Body Posture is imperative in sales. A slouching shoulder with eyes looking on the ground can indicate lack of interest. Standing straight with your weight balanced on each foot indicates you a more assured and relaxed. Always maintain a straight body, whether standing or seated.

- Match an open posture with a genuine facial expression. Dispose of the sunglasses. The customer may think you are hiding something, as they cannot see your eyes, be transparent and avoid piercing looks this can intimidate.

- When doing sales calls and presentations, use sincere and open body language. Never cross the arms. The outward and upward gestures of hands useful and express openness.

- Leaning back on a chair with hands placed at the back of the head, may drive customers away as this indicates arrogance and a false sense of confidence. Hands on the waist, however, exudes positive confidence.

- Do not point. Pointing is an aggressive act that can be interpreted as hostility, avoid this gesture if you really want to sell.

- Signs that indicate someone is open for negotiations and are willing to compromise are: Unbuttoning the jacket indicates one is ready to talk and to listen to a counter offer.

Removing the jacket or rolling sleeves up indicates they are ready to decide or to give in to the final price.

Use body language to recognize and counteract potential objections:

- If the customer's arms are crossed, it indicates disinterest. Use a pattern interrupt such as passing a brochure over, the customer will uncross to take the paperwork. When arms and legs are uncrossed, and hands are open, this is the best scenario, as they are open to your ideas…and a sale is more likely to happen.

- When a customer mimics your gestures such as you fix your hair and they follow. It indicates the customer is very receptive to your ideas and open to buy your idea or product. If this is the case, stop pitching, and close the sale.

- If the customer covers their mouth, touches the nose, or near the eye, there is a probability that you are losing the sale. Something you said or did may have discouraged them. Repeat the sales process yet this time, do it differently and encourage the customer to open up and share ideas. Open your palms and occasionally place it to your chest (this signifies honesty).

- When the customer shows interest through body movements, close the sale.

Every effort should be made to earn the trust of the customer, to ultimately close the deal. If you are unable to close the sale, be professional and gracious at all times. Thank the customer for listening and shake their hand with sincerity. Sales are not always achieved on first meetings. Closing the presentation on a positive note will leave a good impression. They may still be your next positive customer at another time or refer others to you.

Use your body every way you can in the selling process. Body movements can transform prospects to become believers in the offerings. Be enthusiastic and if you truly believe in the quality of your product or service, others will intuitively feel it.

Chapter 16
Body Language in Job Interviews

Gone are the days when the job seeker has to write the handwritten application to earn that job interview. In this age of computers and cyber technology, most employers prefer applicants who apply online, and more job seekers are looking to the net for their job opportunities. But one thing remains the same - the body language of the applicant during job interviews and how they make the first impression as they step inside that interview room.

Leave a lasting impression

Based on your body language, an interviewer may know whether you are confident or not, if you are shy, friendly, a loner, a team player, or even if you are telling the truth. The interviewer generally observes responses that match the qualifications. They can determine if you are capable of handling the job, whether you are devoted, or how you interact with others. They will not only pay attention to answers from questions, how you say it will be noted.

Punctuality

This is the most important aspect of the job interview, arriving on time. A job interview is deemed as a very important appointment and being late is a cardinal crime that may cause you to lose the opportunity. Your attitude regarding time will relay a message and will indicate your professionalism as well as your determination. It is better to be early by one hour than to be a minute late.

First Encounter

When the interviewer enters do not offer your hand for a handshake unless they offer their hand. Shake hands firmly, but do not squeeze and maintain eye contact.

Body Posture

Good body posture during job interviews are imperative. At the beginning of the interview, sit up straight with your back leaning against the back of a chair. Do not slouch or move sideways on the chair because it might be perceived as a lack of interest or boredom. Sitting on the edge of a chair can indicate that you are a little nervous and that you feel uneasy with the situation. When the interviewer speaks, lean forward a little. This shows interest and attention in what is being verbalized also tilt your head a little to show that you are listening closely.

Gestures

Do not cross your arms this is defensive expression. Place your hands loosely upon your lap or on the armrest of your chair. By doing this, you will also be able to make hand movements to support what you are saying. While speaking, nod your head occasionally to expound on a subject or to give more meaning to what you are saying. Hand movements can also help to enhance the conversation. Hand gestures will indicate to interviewer that you are comfortable with the interview process. However, too much hand movement at the beginning of the interview is not suitable, express them gradually throughout the interview.

Observe the hand gestures of the interviewer. If they use their hands a lot to make a point or to clarify something, you can do the same thing (remember mirroring). When the movements stop, do the same. It is important to adjust your gestures to that of the interviewer to establish rapport. Be alert to automatic and unintentional gestures that you may express due to tension. Some gestures that may irritate the interviewer include: Tapping fingers across the desk. Shuffling feet. Nail biting. Toying with a pen.

Eye Contact

Eye contact during an interview has been repeatedly found to have a powerful influence on the interviewer. When you hold good eye contact this receives more favourable hiring decisions, and you are rated more suitable for jobs requiring self-confidence.

The most appropriate eye contact in an interview is two to three second bursts followed by looking away. Looking down continuously, avoiding eye contact altogether, or holding extended eye contact can a result in poor judgment. Continuous shifting of the eyes around the room can present as dishonest. Looking toward the door or appearing distracted by what is going on outside will demonstrate your lack of interest in the job.

Panel Interview

Being interviewed by one person can be easy however, a group can be a daunting ordeal, especially when it comes to who you should look at during the interview.

It is important to maintain eye contact with all the interviewers at an equal extent. By looking uniformly at them, you will establish their trust and you will gain composure throughout the interview process.

When one of the interview partners asks or speaks, maintain eye contact until they cease speaking. This will indicate that you are listening attentively. While they is speak, they may also look at the other interviewers, then back to you, this is where you can nod your head to encourage them to continue speaking.

When answering a question, look first at the one who asked and while answering, look at each interviewer. Then direct back to the person who asked the question when you want to prove a point, when you want to emphasize something, and when you are done answering.

Interviewers Body Language

Observing the body language of the interviewer/s is as important as being aware of your own body movements. The body gestures can give you an indication of how well you are doing. This can serve as a signal to change your approach at an early stage before they give the thumbs down. If something displeases the interviewers, they show their annoyance through body language. When they sigh, shake their heads, look down, or fold arms and lean back, this indicates discontentment or irritability. The may not consciously notice their body language, therefore you still have a chance to shift your strategy.

Being Nervous is Okay

Knowing how to act confidently using body language can increase your chances of passing the interview. You can use this understanding to conceal your anxiety however, this is something of no concern. Many applicants are tense during an interview, and it is normal to be nervous at this stage. Nervousness can indicate how valuable the job is to you. If you present as a happy-go-lucky person, you might be perceived as someone who is not very interested in the job. The interview functions as a way of determining who among the applicants is most capable of performing the job well, yet, it is also a first encounter between individuals, therefore, due to subconscious patterns, nervousness can be felt by all.

Chapter 17
Body Language in Meetings

Communication occurs constantly in a meeting. Not many are involved in speaking, yet everyone expresses body language signals that divulge what they are actually feeling inside. If you are the leader of a meeting, it is important to know if the attendees are interested in what you are saying, or if they agree with your ideas. Early detection of boredom or disagreement is crucial in order for you to change your approach or present a different proposal when necessary.

When most of the attendees recline back in their chairs or stare blankly without blinking an eye, it indicates they are not interested in the topic being discussed. Do not prolong the discussion and do something that will break the monotony. When the attendees nod constantly, it indicates they agree with what you are saying. If they cross the arms, touch the nose or mouth, sit back, and worse, shake the heads, they oppose your ideas. Time to think of some countermeasures to neutralise the situation. When an attendee breathes deeply, this indicates that they want to interrupt the conversation and express a point of view.

Other body gestures to observe: Changing the pitch of the voice. Frowning. Looking down at the ground. Drumming fingers in the table. Exiting the meeting room.

Attempt to detect the inner feelings of each attendee and bear in mind how this can affect the reaction of the other attendees. Emotions can exhibit key facial expressions and body gestures. Recognizing them early in the meeting can prevent any undesirable emotional outbreak to occur. If the topic being discussed becomes "over heated," it might be better to re-schedule the meeting to another time.

Eye Contact

Eye language is important in business as it can often be more indicative of intent rather than other body language. The most effective use of eye contact is in fleeting glances, as prolonged eye contact can be seen as rude, untrustworthy, threatening or even aggressive. Poor eye contact or prolonged periods of looking away can mean the reverse; indifference or outright disinterest. This is why brief glances followed by looking away, or at the material at hand, is most appropriate.

Positioning of eyes can give you indication of what a person is thinking. Generally, a person is passively receiving information if they are simply looking straight ahead and when honestly processing the information they will look upward.

Here are eye movement patterns and what they mean in relation to business:

Eyes focused straight ahead – passive receiving of information

Prolonged eye contact – threat and aggression or disinterest in sales pitch

Eyes to the right – message is being considered

Eyes to the left – person is relating to a past experience.

Eyes down – emotional concentration from an emotional thinker.

Extended looks away – desire to withdraw or vacate.

Eyes at ceiling – conscious analysing.

By being aware of the manner in which the eyes focus, you can gauge the success or failure of the meeting.

Chapter 18
Heart-To-Heart Body Language

Open body language signals comfort, welcome and friendliness. These are signals that you should expresses when you first meet someone, particularly during the introduction. To express open body language, remember to go heart-to-heart. Something almost magical occurs when you open your body language to another person, and when you go heart-to-heart, you are using your body to create a sense of connection.

How to Connect Heart-to-Heart

Connecting heart-to-heart is powerful, and easy to do.

This is where you directly face another from a comfortable distance, with nothing in between you, and there is a direct line between your heart and their heart. Uncross your arms and take hands out of pockets so there's nothing blocking your chest. Focus on another and be open to the interaction.

Imagine an invisible laser shining out of your heart, allow it to flow across to land close to their heart.

When you make the effort to go heart-to-heart, you signal to the other that they have your full attention and that you are welcoming or friendly. This goes a long way in helping another feel comfortable with you and in creating a great first impression.

Chapter 19
Body Language
Love and Lust

Through studies it has been determined that courtship signals are completely unconscious. The more you consciously understand the signals, the better and more successful you will be when courting the one of your desire.

For success in attaining the attention of another, we have to feel good about ourself first. Be confident and natural, otherwise it appears deceitful or desperate. Flirting can be used in many ways, not just in attracting an intimate partner. This can be described as appropriate flirting where level of comfort is considered and applied for the receiver; and this should be done with precise understanding of what you really want, coupled with positive sensations for all included.

Here are some examples for appropriate flirting:
- Don't worry about whether you are making a good impression or not. Instead, analyse how you can make the other feel good. By doing this, you will get the feedback you are expecting and soon you will make the connection.

- Flirting can aid in making friends, or to impress a client as this can indicate that you are more approachable. Wear a smile, as it gives you an aura of being friendly.

- Remember that you cannot attract people just by sitting or standing like a statue. There may be circumstances when you encounter a person who gets a little too close for comfort. You can avoid this by observing the signals: mouth gets larger, the lips swell, eyes widen, pupils dilate, skin flushes and changes colour, or muscles around the mouth move.

- Be persistent. Flirting works best when you are patient. This gives room for improvement if at first you are not getting the results you desire. Try different approaches until you attain what works best for you.

- Practice in the mirror, only then can you make it perfect. This is especially true for meeting friends and prospects, because flirting may involve unwanted actions and attention which can affect interpretation. By watching your reflection, you can pick up on automatic gestures.

- Make the first move! Let go of inhibitions and those ridiculous fears, these do not serve you for the better. Remember to apply positive, appropriate flirting. Who knows it may be the gateway towards the fulfillment of your dreams.

Let Your Body Attract

Do you know why some seem to have an easier time attracting another? Here are some examples to gain attention from someone that interests you;

- Smile sincerely and frequently. In an article by Allen Thompson, *"The Six Don Juan Commandments of Body Language,"* he wrote that smiling is *"The simplest, most obvious, and most powerful of the body language commandments."* He also mentions that *"Smiling conveys, both instantly and clearly, many wonderful things about yourself. Smiling demonstrates confidence, friendliness, a positive attitude, a good mood, and it gives the impression that you're someone who is, most likely, fun to be with. It's also very difficult to ignore."*

- Have a sense of humor. Learn to laugh at yourself as well as at petty matters. People love to be with those who can turn any situation into an entertaining occasion.

- Maintain eye contact. Your eyes are expressive. When you look at another constantly, you express sincere intentions. Eye contact also establishes a bond between people and this helps to feel more natural and comfortable in each other's company.

- Nod your head this will signify your approval and encourage the other to continue talking. You give reassurance that they are presenting well.

- Express open body language. Uncross arms or avoid placing objects such as a food or a cup between the two of you, place these slightly to the left or right. Place your hands on your sides and hold your palms up to convey openness.

Indications of interest from the other

Is this special someone interested in you as well? You see someone, and your heart starts to beat faster. You continue to look at them with confidence to indicate you are interested. Then you wait for a reaction. They may be a bit shy, therefore, they do not look back at you, and this is okay as it is natural if they shift their glance. Here is how to know if they are attracted to you;

- If they look down and away, they are interested.
- Looking to the left or right, there is no interest.

What body language can indicate attraction?
Someone is flirting if they express the following signals:
- The lips show the way. They present a big smile with teeth exposed and the face is relaxed, no worry lines or creases on the forehead. They may gently bite the bottom lip or show the tongue such as; licking lips and touching the front teeth.
- Eyes show you everything. They look at you with a deep stare and pupils are dilated. They raise eyebrows

seductively, may wink from a distance, or when talking with you; and the strongest indicator they blink their eyes more than usual and eyelashes flutter.

- They stroke their hair, comb fingers through the hair, twirl some around the fingers, or they throw the hair back off the shoulders (this is another indication of open body language).

- More skin is revealed, exposing legs, chests or wrists, and they may groom more than usual by tidying their clothes.

- They sit with open legs or cross the legs in a posture for thighs to be seen. Legs may also rub against each other or against the leg of the table.

- Hands mirror feelings. They rub their wrists up and down in a suggestive manner. Rub the chin or touch the cheek, and some may unconsciously touch their chest or breasts. Objects on the table are played with such as; fondling keys, or gently rubbing a drinking glass.

Overall, they maintain eye contact, smile frequently, and exhibit levels of confidence.

Conversation openers

To start a relationship, you must initiate the dialogue. Ask about experiences, such as, "Have you ever tried to...?" or "have you ever gone to...?' Find out what interests them. Compliment in-between conversations, not at the start. Always stay calm and relaxed. Be curious and interested. Nod to indicate that you are listening.

Power of the touch

A simple touch to the body can have numerous meanings depending on how someone perceives touch in body language. For most touch is a basic need, being stroked or general physical contact can transmute a mood, create confidence or comfort. Touch can convey respect and trust and is a way to differentiate power between people. Touching in body language can be powerful when done with strategy, precision, and with accuracy as the art of touching relays signals to the others.

Timing is important, as some will react negatively when touched too soon or too much, based on the circumstances and the mood. For example; when first meeting someone you have interest in, immediate touch can be offensive and viewed as desperate.

Location of touch is another important aspect, for example; touching the arm between the shoulders and elbow is considered appropriate contact, other parts of the body such as legs, abdomen or lower back can be forthcoming and creates discomfort. Touching the middle back or the back of shoulders can indicate support.

You can determine the appropriateness of your touch and what adjustment is required by how the receiver reacts to it. If the person leans in or moves closer to you, this will indicate that you made the right move. However, if the person backs away, even slightly, they indicate that the touch was not appropriate for them, therefore an adjustment is required.

Conclusion

Undeniably, communication is as important as sustaining life with water and food. Even primitive man found ways to communicate needs and desires in order to simplify their existence. In our modern, fast paced and abundant era, its necessity even more so. The world would be chaotic without communication.

There are many channels of communication yet understanding non-verbal communication is the most valuable of all, not only is it fifty five percent of how we communicate to each other, it also reveals the hidden thoughts and feelings of others and more so, your own that stand in the way to successful outcomes.

We are all expressing non-verbal communication, yet we hardly notice that we are doing it; and this is the most reliable sources of truthful information. You have now attained this valuable knowledge to better life experiences. Here are some reminders that you learned: What it really means to read people. First four minutes that can create life-long impression. The keystones of body language. The importance of context, bundling and intuition, our beacon body, along with being mindful of pre-conceived beliefs. How the mind mirrors through neurons and the body and brain are linked. The importance of the limbic systems and in creating honest body language, and the feet are the most honest part of the body. Our ability to reach others through remote intention. The flow of silent speech. Indications of invitation. How posture portrays confidence, or lack in confidence. Our inherent mind strings. The importance of touch. Why environment, conditioned beliefs and the vibration influences body language. Indicators of invasion with personal space, and appropriate distance. How eyes, pupils, blink rate and the mouth can indicate thoughts and emotions. How NLP can help us predict things. What smiles and laughter, can do for others including ourselves. What gestures indicate an open or closed mind and how to overcome a closed body. Why time is obstructive, and how to transmute energy, one example being pattern interrupts...and more.

What you have learned from this book will be beneficial to you in every activity you engage in. Read this book over and over again so that you may master your inherent skills. Use this book as a reference to aid in opening body language for others, and more importantly for yourself. Use the knowledge to unveil your subconscious blocks, or the conditioned beliefs that interfere with attaining the life you desire.

Keep this in mind: Learning body language does not stop here. Experience is the key. Experience will sharpen your body language skills to greater heights, your own non-verbal communication will express consistency and your efficiency will bloom rapidly. Practice, observe and apply the knowledge you have gained. A better life experience awaits you. You are the Alchemist.

To Download your FREE accompanying A-Z Dictionary of Gestures and Non-verbal Cues

go to:

www.perpelflame.com

About the Author

Termina listed as a global Self-Help expert and Author also known as 'The Happy Magnet' has the uncanny ability to tilt the odds so the best will happen resides with her family in Australia and believes in navigating the changing world of experiences.

As an Expansion Mentor and with a corporate background in personal development, design and business, Termina holds a range of qualifications including Transformational Leadership, Public Speaking and Medicine. Also an exponent of Feng Shui, Termina uses her knowledge of Energy and Quantum physics to support individuals and organizations by increasing their success in financial situations, relationships, health or inspiration. Termina loves to use her imagination and has gained the title 'Master of Imagination', she has used her skills to work on many residential and commercial projects, including an open design radio station, Fox Studios and a variety of set designs, where her own artwork was exhibited for TV and film.

Termina holds the knowledge of communication in high acclaim in particular non-verbal language as this has been an exceptional skill in moving her towards her chosen goals. Termina has worked with many great minds including Bob Proctor and Peggy McColl; and adds that seeking knowledge, self-improvement and possibilities through mentors and books is the greatest gift to ourselves.

Termina also believes imagination is the source of advantage, and everybody has the good fortune of this ability, and her book, Festival of the Imagination, is one of her many non-fiction titles which explores this all-important subject.

Festival of the Imagination is one of many non-fiction books by Termina. Termina calls herself a student of self-actualization. It was through her studies and introspection practices that she was able to tap into her unique soul signature and states that she is guided by source. *"At all times we carry with us all the answers. There is nothing in the physical world that will truly give us the ultimate answer; our unique soul print and purpose in life; and it is because of this only ourself has the true answers for what makes us happy or why we are here. We only require external tools, or mentors to get us started and guide us in a direction towards connecting with our soul's voice. With the right tools and mentors, we are on our way to unleashing our true, powerful self."*

Termina credits communication and self-actualization practices for her success and harmony in her life. Another one she credits is Feng Shui as a guide to alignment for choices. *"It was through my studies and practice of Feng shui that I discovered the importance this ancient art plays in our life. 33% of our experiences are created through our physical visualization board, our environment. When we apply the principles of Feng Shui our lives become the choices we desire, we are in control of our own experiences at all times and good fortune is attainable. Through Feng Shui I have seen improvements and successes in my own life along with the many others who have appointed my services."*

For more information about this author
And other books:
www.terminaashton.com
www.terminafengshui.com
www.perpelflame.com
www.thehappymagnet.com